Internal Migration in Sri Lanka
and Its Social Consequences

About the Book and Authors

The South Asian nation of Sri Lanka has experienced a
tremendous amount of internal migration in recent decades.
More than two million persons, nearly one out of seven, were
born in districts other than their place of enumeration for
the 1981 census. The authors of this book probe the aspects
of internal migration in Sri Lanka and some of the lesser-
known social and political consequences of these population
shifts. Three major aspects of societal upheavals related
to internal migration are examined: unbalanced sex ratios,
rising rates of suicide, and increased ethnic conflict. The
linkages between these provide a new and provocative approach
to understanding some of the unanticipated effects of social
change.

Sri Lanka provides an instructive case study of the
rapid transition from a settled agrarian society to a more
complex and differentiated one and of the demographic and
political sequelae that accompany such a change.

Robert N. Kearney is professor of political science at
the Maxwell School, Syracuse University, and has written
extensively on politics and society in Sri Lanka. His
current research interests center on aspects of rapid social
change in Sri Lanka. Barbara Diane Miller, an anthropologist,
is senior research associate in the Metropolitan Studies
Program at the Maxwell School, Syracuse University. She has
done research on children's health and women's status in
India, local public finance in Bangladesh, and low-income
households in Jamaica.

Internal Migration in Sri Lanka and Its Social Consequences

Robert N. Kearney
and Barbara Diane Miller

Westview Press / Boulder and London

International Studies in Migration

This Westview softcover edition is printed on acid-free paper and bound in
softcovers that carry the highest rating of the National Association of
State Textbook Administrators, in consultation with the Association of
American Publishers and the Book Manufacturers' Institute.

Published in 1987 in the United States of America by Westview Press, Inc.;
Frederick A. Praeger, Publisher; 5500 Central Avenue, Boulder, Colorado
80301

Library of Congress Cataloging-in-Publication Data
Kearney, Robert N.
   Internal migration in Sri Lanka and its social
consequences.
   (International studies in migration)
   1. Migration, Internal--Sri Lanka. 2. Sri Lanka--
Social conditions. I. Miller, Barbara D., 1948-   .
II. Title. III. Series.
HB2096.8.A3K39 1987   304.8'09549'3   86-18989
ISBN 0-8133-7321-2

Composition for this book was provided by the authors.
This book was produced without formal editing by the publisher.

Printed and bound in the United States of America

The paper used in this publication meets the requirements of the
American National Standard for Permanence of Paper for Printed
Library Materials Z39.48-1984.

6   5   4   3   2   1

Contents

List of Tables and Figures   ix

Preface   xiii

1   PATTERNS OF INTERNAL MIGRATION IN SRI LANKA . .   1
    Interdistrict Population Movement   3
    Measures of Interdistrict Migration   14
    Sex Ratios as Clues to Migration   18
        Regional Differentials   23
        Growth Rates, Densities, and Sex Ratios . . .   24
        Rural-Urban Migration   27
        Ethnic Patterns   29
    Conclusion   33

2   UNBALANCED SEX RATIOS   39
    Sex Ratio Variations by Age Group   40
        Juveniles   40
        10-19 Year-Olds   45
        20-29 Year-Olds   45
        Older Adults   46
        Summary of the Sex Ratio Data   47
    Data on Migrants in the Population   47
    Sociocultural Correlates   53
        Spouse Separation   57
    Conclusion   59

3   RISING SUICIDE RATES   65
    The Increase in Suicides   66
    District Variations   67
    Sex Differentials   74
    Age Groups   78

Suicide in Selected Districts   80
Migration, Social Disruption, and Suicide . . .   84
Conclusion   85

4   ETHNIC CONFRONTATION   91
The Ethnic Communities of Sri Lanka   91
Migration and the "Tamil Homeland"   94
Ethnic Change in the North and East   96
    Lifetime Migrants   108
    Urbanization   109
Sri Lanka Tamil Population Movement   109
Ethnicity and the Proposed Eelam   113
Conclusion   115

5   FUTURE RESEARCH AND POLICY IMPLICATONS   121
Prospective Research Directions   123
Public Policy Considerations   125
In Conclusion   126

BIBLIOGRAPHY   129

INDEX   139

Tables and Figures

TABLES

1.1 Percentage of 1981 district residents born
    in other districts   4

1.2 Population density (persons per square
    kilometer), by district, 1946, 1971,
    and 1981   7

1.3 Unemployment rates by sex and district, 1981 .   9

1.4 Average annual rates of population growth
    between censuses, by district, 1946-1981 . . .   11

1.5 Urbanization by district, 1981   13

1.6 Interdistrict migration measures derived from
    district of residence and district of birth,
    1971   15

1.7 Districts of origin of the three largest
    streams of lifetime in-migrants, 1971   19

1.8 Districts of destination of the three largest
    streams of lifetime out-migrants, 1971   21

1.9 National sex ratios at censuses of Sri Lanka,
    1871-1981   24

1.10 Sex ratios by district, 1946-1981   25

1.11 Sex ratios for interdistrict migrants by
duration of stay in district of 1971
residence   26

1.12 Sex ratios of migrants by duration of stay
and of non-migrants, cities over 50,000
population, 1971   29

1.13 Sex ratios and proportions of total
population of major ethnic communities,
1946 and 1971   30

1.14 Sex ratios and percentages of population
of major ethnic communities, by district,
1971   31

2.1 Sex ratio at birth, 1960-1979 (live
births)   41

2.2 Sex ratios by district and 10-year age
groups, 1971   42

2.3 District population not born in the
district, by sex and age, 11 selected
districts, 1971   48

2.4 Labor participation rate, literacy rate,
and singulate mean age at marriage, Sri
Lanka, 1971   54

2.5 Simple correlation coefficients between
district sex ratios and sociocultural
variables, 1971   55

2.6 Spouse separation rates for selected
districts, 1971   58

3.1 Numbers and rates of suicides, 1950-1980 . . .   68

3.2 Suicide rates by district, selected years . .   70

3.3 Approximate suicide rates by district
and sex, selected years   75

3.4 Suicide rates by sex and age group,
selected years   79

3.5 Selected districts, with migration
    characteristics   80

3.6 Approximate suicide rates by age group and
    sex, selected districts, 1980   82

4.1 Ethnic composition of Sri Lanka district
    populations, 1981 (percent)   93

4.2 Ethnic composition of northern and eastern
    district populations, 1911-1981 (percent) . .   97

4.3 Population changes by ethnic community,
    northern and eastern districts, 1946-1981 . .   99

4.4 Ethnic composition of Batticaloa and
    Amparai district populations, 1963, 1971,
    and 1981 (percent)   102

4.5 Population born in districts other than that
    of 1981 enumeration, by region/district of
    birth (percent), northern and eastern
    districts   106

4.6 Urbanization by ethnic community, northern
    and eastern districts, 1981 (percent of
    community)   107

4.7 Ethnic composition of population of
    Sri Lanka, selected census years,
    1911-1981 (percent)   110

4.8 Percentage distribution of Sri Lanka Tamil
    population by province, 1911, 1946, 1971,
    and 1981   111

4.9 Population of the region associated with
    the proposed Eelam (Jaffna, Mannar,
    Vavuniya, Mullaitivu, Trincomalee, and
    Batticaloa districts), by ethnic
    community, 1981   114

FIGURES

1.1 Sri Lanka, administrative districts at the
    time of the 1981 census   6

1.2 Sri Lanka, administrative districts at the
    time of the 1971 census   17

1.3 Districts by population density, 1981;
    population growth rate, 1971-1981; and
    sex ratio, 1981 (excluding Colombo and
    Gampaha districts)   27

1.4 Locations of districts with highest and
    lowest sex ratios depicted in Figure 1.3 . . .   28

2.1 Colombo, Galle, and Polonnaruwa districts,
    A: migrants as a percentage of age groups
    by sex, and B: sex ratios of migrants by
    age groups   51

3.1 Suicide rates by sex, 1950-1980   69

3.2 Average suicide rate, 1971-1980, and
    average annual population growth rate,
    1971-1981, by district   73

3.3 Suicide rates by sex and age group,
    Sri Lanka, 1980   78

4.1 Districts of the northern and eastern
    provinces, showing Sri Lanka Tamil
    proportions of district populations,
    1911, 1946, and 1981   104

4.2 Districts of the northern and eastern
    provinces, showing Sinhalese proportions of
    district populations, 1911, 1946, and 1981 . .   105

4.3 Sri Lanka, showing provincial boundaries . . .   112

Preface

Few studies of migration address the topics of sex ratio imbalances, suicide, and ethnic conflict. Our analysis of Sri Lanka is unorthodox because it pushes the study of internal migration far beyond its conventional boundaries toward an understanding of some disquieting sequelae of population movement within the island. We attempt to chart linkages between the massive population changes created by internal migration, much of which is sponsored by state programs, and the breaking up of families, the increase in self-destructive behavior, and the rise in ethnic tensions. The conclusions appear particularly disturbing when one remembers that Sri Lanka is a "showcase" of modernization in Asia, with bounteous natural beauty, a highly literate population, dramatically declining mortality rates, and an impressive record of democracy.

This monograph is unusual in another way because it is presumably not common for a political scientist and an anthropologist to undertake a joint study of internal migration. Our common interest in social change in South Asia brought us together for this work. It is also probably not usual for a study to grow in the manner of a coral reef from a work originally conceived as consisting of three tables, three maps, and ten pages of discussion to one that could be described as monographic. A brief history of how this volume came to be may help the reader understand why it comprises such seemingly disparate topics as sex ratios, suicides, and ethnic tensions. For us, this book was a journey of discovery--and the major discovery was that we were in fact writing a book.

The study which eventuated in this volume began in a very unportentous way. At the beginning of the 1982 spring semester, Kearney agreed to talk on the subject of "Women in Sri Lanka" at Syracuse University's weekly Women's Studies Seminar. In preparation for the talk, he calculated sex ratios by district and was struck by the much greater than anticipated variations between districts and the clear regional patterns that emerged. The districts with high (male-preponderant) sex ratios also had high population growth rates and low population densities. Having no previous experience with the study of migration and sex ratios, he sought assistance from Miller. From this initial discussion emerged the idea of a brief collaborative paper that would "practically write itself."

The first major escalation of the study was a consequence of the richness of the 1971 census data, which proved to be addictive. The simple examination of sex ratios in relation to internal migration led to more and more analysis. Later in the year, Miller organized a panel on the subject of sex-differentials in internal migration for the 1983 Annual Meeting of the Association for Asian Studies, for which we agreed to write a paper on sex-differential patterns of migration within Sri Lanka.

An extensive reworking of the paper presented at the 1983 meetings resulted in a lengthy version that appeared in Peasant Studies in 1983.[1] The innumerable ways in which the census data could be aggregated, disaggregated, and reaggregated, producing ever more fascinating results, continued to cast a hypnotic spell. Another substantial revision and enlargement of the paper was published in 1984 in the Women in International Development Working Paper Series produced at Michigan State University.[2]

An intervening study of suicide in Sri Lanka by Kearney and Miller hinted at tantalizing links between suicide and migration.[3] The role of migration as an issue in the political conflict between Sinhalese and Tamils had long interested Kearney, and he found irresistable the possibilities of charting shifts in the ethnic composition of regions from the census materials. Also, data from the 1981 census were becoming available.

In the spring of 1985, the book began to emerge. It was originally conceived as three separate essays on elements of internal migration in Sri Lanka, collected in the form of a very brief volume. The plan continued to grow beyond the original conception in scope and in length for several months thereafter until late 1985 when we, with determination, called a halt to our creativity. We were, incidentally, still looking for the section that would practically write itself.

This work might be characterized as a product of enthusiatic empiricism. We began without fixed preconceptions of the findings and conclusions we would reach and generally without commitment to a theoretical proposition or methodology. We followed where the data led. Our inspiration came from Abraham Maslow's eloquent contention: "Facts just don't lie there like pancakes, just doing nothing; they are to a certain extent signposts which tell you what to do, which make suggestions to you, which nudge you in one direction rather than another."[4] We received a great number of nudges from census and other materials. Some of our eventual conclusions--the more somber ones in particular--were unexpected products of our explorations of the data.

It seems that, with all this work devoted to the study of internal migration in Sri Lanka, the subject must be as exhausted as we are. But in writing the last chapter, ostensibly a conclusion, we realized that instead we have succeeded in opening up new beginnings for further research and more in-depth thinking on the unexpected consequences of population movement in Sri Lanka. We hope that, in any case, this work may help to stimulate some rethinking and further searching examination of social and personal consequences of migration within Sri Lanka and other contemporary nations faced with similar rapid social change.

Throughout the several years during which this book grew, we were assisted by numerous persons. In Sri Lanka, the directors of the Department of Census and Statistics, W.A.A.S. Peiris and his successor, R.B. Korale, and the department's staff were very helpful in providing access to published and unpublished data. Data on suicide were obtained with the assistance of A.K. Ramanathapillai and the personnel of the Department of the Registrar-General's statistical branch. Several persons read one or more chapters at various stages of development and offered advice for improvement: the late David Sopher of Syracuse University, Hanna Papanek of Boston University, Josef Gugler of the University of Connecticut, Gananath Obeyesekere of Princeton University, and Stanley Tambiah of Harvard University.

Institutional support from Syracuse University took many forms. The special contributions made by Cherie

Ackerson, Martha Bonney, Esther Gray, and Stephanie Waterman of the Metropolitan Studies Program must be mentioned first. They typed and revised innumerable versions of all the chapters and their very high level of skill helped make the project move more quickly than it would have otherwise. Richard Joseph, Research Associate in the Metropolitan Studies Program, provided assistance with the statistical analyses. The preparation of the maps and figures was done by the Syracuse University Cartographic Laboratory under the capable direction of D. Michael Kirchoff. The Foreign and Comparative Studies Program provided financial assistance for the artwork.

Robert N. Kearney
Barbara Diane Miller

NOTES

1. Robert N. Kearney and Barbara D. Miller, "Sex-Differential Patterns of Internal Migration in Sri Lanka," Peasant Studies X, Summer 1983, pp. 224-250.

2. Robert N. Kearney and Barbara D. Miller, "Sex Differences in Patterns of Internal Migration in Sri Lanka," Women in International Development Working Paper Series No. 44 (East Lansing, MI: Michigan State University, Office of Women in International Development, 1984).

3. Robert N. Kearney and Barbara D. Miller, "The Spiral of Suicide and Social Change in Sri Lanka," Journal of Asian Studies XLV, November 1985, pp. 81-101.

4. Abraham H. Maslow, The Farther Reaches of Human Nature (New York: Viking Press, 1971), p. 27.

1

Patterns of Internal Migration in Sri Lanka

Internal migration, or population movement within a nation's boundaries, is an important component of population dynamics and is related to many features of social change such as urbanization, industrialization, government land settlement policies, agricultural innovations, literacy, and evolving family structures.[1] The South Asian nation of Sri Lanka has been the scene of a great deal of internal migration over recent decades.[2] At the census of 1981 more than two million persons, nearly one of every seven, were born in districts other than the district of 1981 enumeration.[3]

The movement of population within the nation constitutes one facet of the wide-ranging demographic and social change that Sri Lanka has been experiencing. A sharp drop in the death rate after 1945 was followed by a period of very rapid population growth. Between 1945 and 1960 the death rate per 1,000 population fell from 21.9 to 12.6.[4] The national population climbed from under 6,660,000 in 1946 to nearly 12,700,000 in 1971, an increase of more than 90 percent in a quarter of a century. By the 1960s, however, the rate of population growth had slackened considerably. In the decade 1971-1981 the average annual rate of population growth was 1.7, down from 2.8 in 1946-1953. The 1981 census enumerated a population of slightly less than 15 million persons.[5]

The chapters in this volume probe features of internal migration in Sri Lanka and some of the social and political consequences of these population shifts. Compared to the attention devoted to social determinants of migration in the demographic literature, relatively little has been done on the social consequences of population movement, particularly of voluntary migration.[6]

This volume examines aspects of certain social developments that have accompanied internal migration in Sri Lanka: unbalanced sex ratios, rising rates of suicide, and increased ethnic conflict. These topics are not the usual subject matter included in studies of internal migration, but we feel that they are important topics associated with migration not only in contemporary Sri Lanka but probably in many other countries as well. Sri Lanka offers the promise of an instructive case study of transition from a relatively stable agrarian, village society to a more complex and differentiated one in which many conventional patterns and commonalities of association and belief are being altered or eroded. It has been generally recognized that rapid social change can be disruptive and stressful. The experience of contemporary Sri Lanka suggests that the disruptions and unanticipated or unwanted accompaniments of social change may be considerably more extensive and carry a higher social and personal cost than has been commonly assumed. The case of Sri Lanka may, at the least, signal the advisibility of looking sharply at the variety of unanticipated and undesired accompaniments of migration and other elements of social change in nations undergoing rapid societal transformations.

This introductory chapter explores the general patterns and dimensions of internal migration over recent years and seeks to identify characteristics of internal population movement by focusing on the differences in migration patterns between males and females. In the absence of more direct measures, we rely heavily on sex ratios as indicators of migration. Chapter 2 more intensively probes regional and age-specific sex ratio imbalances resulting from migration and suggests possible areas of personal or social stress resulting from marked distortions of sex ratios. In Chapter 3 the startling phenomenon of a steep rise in the incidence of suicide, with wide variations in suicide rates between districts, is examined against the backdrop of extensive internal movement of population. Chapter 4 discusses migration as an issue in the political confrontation between ethnic communities on the island and the degree to which migration has contributed to an altering of the association between ethnic community and territory. In the final chapter we draw together findings presented in the previous chapters and offer some concluding comments.

The internal migration discussed in this volume is interdistrict migration. Since movement within the nation has generally been unrestricted, the only available gauge of internal migration comes from census figures on lifetime migration--persons residing in districts other than their district of birth. This measure understates the full dimensions of migration since it does not take into account intervening migrations to other districts or migration from and subsequent return to the district of birth. For the present study data are drawn from the censuses of 1911, 1946, 1963, 1971, and 1981, with principal reliance placed on the latter two censuses. We utilize data from the 1981 census whenever possible, but for many of our purposes we rely on materials from the census of 1971 because results from the 1981 census remain incomplete. Census and other demographic data on Sri Lanka have long been regarded as quite reliable and considerably better than similar data for most other developing countries of Asia.[7]

The principal unit of analysis is the district, created for purposes of governmental administration, which also serves as a major reporting unit for census and other demographic and socioeconomic information. Comparisons of district data over time are complicated by changes that have occurred in the number and boundaries of districts. From the census of 1911 through that of 1953, 19 districts existed and information was also reported separately for Chilaw, which ceased being an administrative district in 1909.[8] By the census of 1963, three new districts of Polonnaruwa, Monaragala, and Amparai had been created and reporting for the former district of Chilaw was discontinued. Prior to the 1981 census, new districts of Mullaitivu and Gampaha were created and adjustments were made in the boundaries of several other districts. In order to facilitate comparisons over time, we have in some instances combined districts in order to create or approximate the territory of an earlier district, as will be indicated.

INTERDISTRICT POPULATION MOVEMENT

A preliminary indication of the general extent of interdistrict migration may be gained from Table 1.1, which presents by district the proportion of persons whose usual residence in 1981 was in the district but who were born in other districts (for the location of districts at the

TABLE 1.1

Percentage of 1981 district residents born in other districts[a]

District[b]	Males	Females	Total
Polonnaruwa	52.2	43.7	48.4
Mullaitivu	45.8	39.5	42.8
Vavuniya	41.2	36.1	38.8
Monaragala	31.0	27.2	29.4
Anuradhapura	28.2	23.2	25.9
Trincomalee	24.2	19.7	22.1
Mannar	25.8	17.3	21.9
Colombo	21.5	17.6	19.6
Puttalam	16.9	15.6	16.2
Amparai	18.0	14.0	16.1
Matale	16.3	15.9	16.1
Gampaha	15.1	15.0	15.0
Nuwara Eliya	13.3	13.2	13.2
Hambantota	13.1	11.6	12.4
Ratnapura	12.6	10.5	11.6
Kalutara	9.6	10.5	10.1
Kurunegala	9.1	9.6	9.3
Kandy	7.5	8.0	7.8
Badulla	7.8	7.1	7.5
Kegalle	5.8	8.1	7.0
Matara	5.6	6.3	6.0
Galle	5.4	5.9	5.7
Batticaloa	5.5	4.2	4.9
Jaffna	3.6	2.8	3.2
All Districts	14.1	12.4	13.3

Source: Derived from Census, 1981, No. 2, Table 18.

[a] Excluding foreign-born persons and those whose place of birth was not stated.

[b] Ordered highest to lowest percentage of total residents in the district born in other districts.

census of 1981, see Figure 1.1). More than one-fifth of the 1981 residents of seven districts were born in other districts, and in only eight districts were less than one-tenth of the residents born outside the district. Nearly half the residents of Polonnaruwa and two out of five residents of Mullaitivu and Vavuniya were born in other districts. The districts with large proportions of residents born elsewhere are located in the island's north-central and northeastern regions. Very low proportions of residents who were born in other districts were found in Matara and Galle on the southern coast and in Batticaloa in the East and Jaffna at the far North of the island.

The dominant pattern of internal migration in Sri Lanka has been the movement of persons from the southwestern Wet Zone to areas of the north-central, northeastern, and eastern Dry Zone. The Wet Zone, located in the southwestern quarter of the island (Figure 1.1), consists of the southwestern and southern coastal plain and a major portion of the central highlands. This region receives an annual rainfall of 100 to 200 inches. Although rain falls throughout the year, much of the Wet Zone's precipitation comes from the southwest monsoon which generally commences in May. The remainder of the island, the broad central plain slanting northward from the central highlands and the northern and eastern coastal plains, are referred to as the Dry Zone, something of a misnomer relative to the arid northwestern regions of the Indian subcontinent. The Dry Zone differs from the Wet Zone by the seasonal pattern of precipitation as well as by the amount of annual rainfall. The Dry Zone generally receives about 50 to 75 inches of rain a year, including precipitation brought by the northeast monsoon which sweeps out of the Bay of Bengal by about November or December.[9]

The crowding of rural populations in the southwestern Wet Zone as a result of population growth, together with the existence of sparsely populated and lightly cultivated land in the Dry Zone, has provided the principal impetus to internal migration.[01] District population densities at the censuses of 1946, 1971, and 1981 appear in Table 1.2. In 1946, densities in the Southwest exceeded 200 persons per square kilometer, whereas in the north-central, northeastern, and eastern Dry Zone they dropped to well below 30. By 1981, island-wide population density had more than doubled due to rapid population growth accompanying a sharp reduction in the death rate after 1945. The pattern of high densities in the Southwest and low densities in the

6

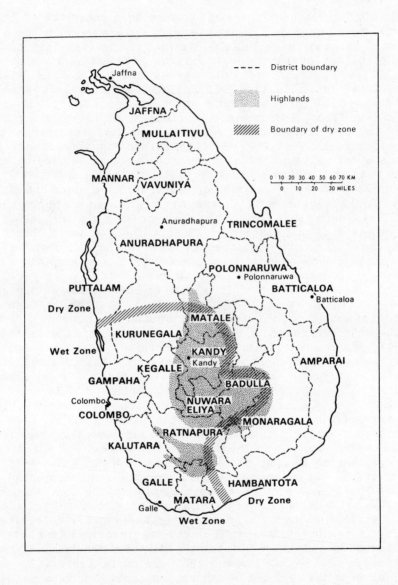

Figure 1.1   Sri Lanka, administrative districts at the time
of the 1981 census

TABLE 1.2

Population density (persons per square kilometer),[a] by district, 1946, 1971, and 1981

District	1946	1971	1981
Colombo	687	1,318	2,603
Gampaha	b	b	993
Matara	286	476	517
Kalutara	286	460	515
Galle	275	445	487
Kandy	304	508	476
Nuwara Eliya	221	371	425
Kegalle	245	398	410
Jaffna	166	284	401
Kurunegala	103	218	254
Ratnapura	107	207	246
Badulla	45	221	228
Matale	68	160	179
Puttalam	61	129	166
Hambantota	58	133	164
Batticaloa	29	106	134
Amparai	c	93	130
Trincomalee	28	73	98
Anuradhapura	14	55	82
Polonnaruwa	d	49	77
Mannar	13	32	53
Monaragala	e	27	39
Mullaitivu	f	f	39
Vavuniya	6	26	36
Sri Lanka	103	198	230

(continued)

TABLE 1.2 (continued)

Source: Derived from Department of Census and Statistics
(Sri Lanka), Statistical Abstract of the Democratic
Socialist Republic of Sri Lanka, 1979 (Colombo: Department
of Government Printing, 1981); and Census, 1981, No. 1.

[a] Excluding inland waters.

[b] Included in Colombo district.

[c] Included in Batticaloa district.

[d] Included in Anuradhapura district.

[e] Included in Badulla district.

[f] Included in Vavuniya district.

North (other than Jaffna) and East remained in 1981.
However, excluding urbanized Colombo and Gampaha districts,
the ratio of highest to lowest district population density
dropped from 48:1 to 14:1 between 1946 and 1981, an
indication of the extent of migration from the densely
populated to the sparsely populated areas.

High and rising rates of unemployment probably
contributed to the movement of persons out of the
southwestern Wet Zone. Unemployment, which was heavily
concentrated among young persons seeking their first jobs,
climbed from 10.5 percent of the labor force in 1959/1960
to 14.3 percent in 1969/1970.[11] The 1981 census reported
an aggregate rate of unemployment of 17.9 percent.
Unemployment rates, however, varied markedly among
districts as is indicated in Table 1.3. Sparsely populated
Mannar registered the lowest rates of unemployment for both
males and females. Mullaitivu, Vavuniya, and Anuradhapura
also had relatively low rates for both sexes. The six
districts with the highest male unemployment rates--Matara,
Galle, Kegalle, Kalutara, Gampaha, and Colombo--are all
clustered in the densely populated southwestern Wet Zone.
Female unemployment rates for these districts were also
above the aggregate national rate for females, although the
correspondence between high unemployment rates in the
Southwest and lower rates in the Dry Zone to the north and
east was less marked for women than for men.

TABLE 1.3
Unemployment rates[a] by sex and district, 1981

District[b]	Males	Females	Total
Mannar	2.5	7.9	3.0
Mullaitivu	4.3	11.8	5.4
Vavuniya	4.1	16.5	6.0
Nuwara Eliya	8.2	8.8	8.5
Anuradhapura	6.2	18.5	8.6
Batticaloa	6.3	31.2	8.8
Badulla	9.0	13.3	10.5
Monaragala	7.9	28.6	10.7
Puttalam	7.2	24.6	10.7
Matale	8.9	23.2	12.3
Trincomalee	9.2	42.5	12.3
Amparai	10.3	33.4	13.6
Polonnaruwa	10.1	38.5	13.9
Ratnapura	11.3	21.2	14.0
Jaffna	9.7	40.8	14.1
Kurunegala	10.3	30.4	14.9
Hambantota	13.4	40.5	18.6
Kandy	13.7	31.0	18.9
Colombo	16.6	35.8	21.5
Kegalle	19.1	40.6	25.1
Kalutara	18.7	42.2	25.3
Galle	20.3	39.2	26.0
Gampaha	18.6	49.3	26.1
Matara	21.3	41.6	27.3
Sri Lanka	13.2	31.8	17.9

Source: Department of Census and Statistics (Sri Lanka), Census of Population and Housing, Sri Lanka, 1981: The Economically Active Population, Tables Based on a Ten Percent Sample, Preliminary Release No. 4 (Colombo: Department of Census and Statistics, 1983), p. x.

[a] Unemployed persons as a percentage of the economically active population (or labor force) ten years of age and older.

[b] Ordered lowest to highest total unemployment rate.

Commencing prior to independence, the government has been developing irrigation schemes and sponsoring migration into sparsely populated Dry Zone areas in the eastern and north-central portions of the island.[12] The near-eradication of malaria in the Dry Zone by the use of DDT after the Second World War removed a major impediment to migration into that area from the increasingly crowded Southwest. In 1970 the government initiated a massive multi-purpose river development project designed to harness the waters of the Mahaweli River, which flows from the central highlands northeasterly through the Dry Zone. The project was designed to bring into intensive cultivation through irrigation 900,000 acres of land previously either untilled or under-utilized, and to make possible the settlement in the Dry Zone of additional large numbers of migrant cultivators from the densely populated areas. The Mahaweli development was originally to be phased over a period of 25 to 30 years, but in 1977 a vastly accelerated schedule was adopted.[13] The Mahaweli project promises to increase the already sizable movement of persons into the Dry Zone, considerably expanding both the economic opportunities and the social dislocations and disruptions attendant on migration.

Average annual rates of district population growth between censuses since 1946 are presented in Table 1.4. Despite the creation of several new districts in the areas of rapid population growth during the 1960s and 1970s, it is evident from Table 1.4 that districts in the north-central, northeastern, and eastern parts of the island, the districts with low population densities, have had high rates of population growth relative to the growth rates of districts in the central, southern, and western regions.

Unlike the situation in many nations of Asia, internal migration in Sri Lanka has not involved large movements of persons from the rural areas to the cities.[14] Rural to urban migration has occurred, especially to the large Colombo conurbation, Jaffna, and Kandy, but the nation has remained predominantly rural. Most of the internal population movement is rural to rural migration. In 1981, urban residents accounted for less than 22 percent of the nation's population, a modest increase over the nearly 16 percent of the population that was classified as urban in 1946.[15] Furthermore, a very large proportion of the urban population is located within and near the Colombo metropolis. In Table 1.5 the urban proportions of district populations and the district's proportion of the total

TABLE 1.4
Average annual rates of population growth between censuses,
by district, 1946-1981

District[a]	1946-1953	1953-1963	1963-1971	1971-1981[b]
Mullaitivu	c	c	c	7.8
Polonnaruwa	d	d	4.5	6.1
Vavuniya	6.0	6.8	4.1	5.9
Anuradhapura	7.4	5.4	4.1	5.1
Monaragala	e	e	4.7	4.5
Mannar	4.7	3.1	3.1	4.4
Amparai	f	f	3.1	4.3
Trincomalee	1.4	5.0	3.8	3.6
Puttalam	3.2	2.8	2.8	3.0
Batticaloa	4.2	4.1	3.3	2.9
Hambantota	3.5	3.5	2.7	2.5
Jaffna	2.1	2.2	1.6	1.9
Gampaha	g	g	g	1.8
Kurunegala	3.7	3.0	2.3	1.8
Ratnapura	3.0	2.5	2.5	1.8
Matale	3.7	2.3	2.6	1.4
Kalutara	2.0	1.8	1.7	1.3
Colombo	2.7	2.5	2.3	1.3
Galle	1.9	2.0	1.6	1.1
Matara	2.3	2.2	1.6	1.0
Kegalle	2.3	2.0	1.3	0.6
Badulla	3.3	3.3	2.1	0.4
Kandy	2.4	2.1	1.6	0.3
Nuwara Eliya	2.8	2.0	1.5	-0.3
Sri Lanka	2.8	2.6	2.2	1.7

(continued)

12

TABLE 1.4 (continued)

Source: Department of Census and Statistics (Sri Lanka), Census of Population, 1971, Vol. II, Part 1 (Colombo: Department of Government Printing, 1975); Census, 1981, No. 2, Table 1.

[a] Ordered highest to lowest growth rate in 1971-1981.

[b] The 1971-1981 growth rates were derived from the population figures reported in Census, 1981, No. 2, Table 1, but in some cases differ from the rates cited in that table.

[c] Included in Vavuniya district.

[d] Included in Anuradhapura district.

[e] Included in Badulla district.

[f] Included in Trincomalee district.

[g] Included in Colombo district.

TABLE 1.5
Urbanization by district, 1981

District	Urban Percentage of District Population	District's Percentage of Total Urban Population
Colombo	74.3	39.5
Jaffna	32.6	8.5
Trincomalee	32.4	2.6
Gampaha	27.8	12.1
Batticaloa	24.0	2.5
Kalutara	21.4	5.5
Galle	20.6	5.3
Vavuniya	19.3	0.6
Amparai	13.8	1.7
Mannar	13.5	0.5
Kandy	13.1	4.6
Puttalam	12.5	1.9
Matara	11.1	2.2
Matale	10.6	1.2
Hambantota	9.8	1.3
Mullaitivu	9.3	0.2
Badulla	8.0	1.6
Polonnaruwa	7.9	0.6
Kegalle	7.8	1.7
Ratnapura	7.4	1.9
Nuwara Eliya	7.3	1.2
Anuradhapura	7.1	1.3
Kurunegala	3.6	1.4
Monaragala	2.2	0.2
Sri Lanka	21.5	100.0

Source: Census, 1981, No. 1, p. 4.

urban population in 1981 are presented. Colombo district
included about 40 percent of Sri Lanka's urban population.
Colombo and adjacent Gampaha districts together (which
until 1978 constituted the single district of Colombo)
accounted for more than half the urban population, nearly
1,650,000 of about 3,195,000 urban residents on the island.

MEASURES OF INTERDISTRICT MIGRATION

That there has been a great deal of interdistrict
movement of population is evident from Table 1.6, which
depicts migration measures by district from the 1971 census
(districts at the time of the 1971 census appear in Figure
1.2). Districts that have experienced large net gains of
population through migration, such as Colombo and
Anuradhapura, have also contributed significant numbers of
out-migrants to other districts. Kurunegala, Ratnapura,
and Matale display relatively low levels of net gain
through migration, but have had large flows of both in- and
out-migration. Even the districts with the largest net
population losses through migration--Galle, Kandy, and
Matara--have had sizable influxes of migrants as well.
Colombo, the metropolitan hub of the island, was the
major recipient of interdistrict migrants. The other
districts with large net gains from migration--
Anuradhapura, Trincomalee, Polonnaruwa, Amparai, and
Monaragala--form a broad arc from the north-central Dry
Zone to the southeastern quarter of the island, all areas
of low population density. Of these five districts, only
Amparai had a 1971 population density exceeding 75 persons
per square kilometer (see Table 1.2).
The major losses of population through migration
appeared in Matara, Galle, Kegalle, and Kalutara districts
of the southwestern Wet Zone, in Kandy in the central
highlands, and in Jaffna at the island's northern tip.
Aside from Jaffna, with a population density of 284, the
other five districts of heavy out-migration all had 1971
population densities approaching or exceeding 400 persons
per square kilometer and ranked after Colombo second
through sixth in magnitude of district population density.
Hence, it can be concluded that the major flow of
interdistrict migration has been from the densely populated
districts, mostly in the southwestern Wet Zone, to the
sparsely populated districts of the Dry Zone. There is a
weak negative correlation between 1971 population density

TABLE 1.6

Interdistrict migration measures derived from district of residence and district of birth, 1971

District[a]	In-Migrants[b]		Out-Migrants[c]		Net Gain or Loss[d]	Lifetime Migration Rate[g]
	Number[d]	Percent[e]	Number[d]	Percent[f]		
Polonnaruwa	78.0	47.7	8.8	8.8	69.7	42.54
Vavuniya	33.0	35.5	4.9	7.5	28.1	29.41
Trincomalee	56.0	29.4	13.9	9.2	42.3	22.05
Monaragala	51.7	27.1	10.8	7.2	40.9	21.35
Anuradhapura	103.3	26.6	24.3	7.9	79.0	20.30
Amparai	57.7	21.3	5.9	2.7	51.8	19.01
Puttalam	74.1	19.6	47.7	13.5	26.4	6.96
Colombo	440.0	16.6	279.4	11.2	160.6	6.02
Hambantota	52.6	15.4	38.9	11.9	13.7	4.02
Kurunegala	141.5	13.8	118.2	11.8	23.2	2.26
Ratnapura	91.8	14.1	83.8	13.1	8.0	1.10
Matale	66.9	21.4	65.9	21.1	1.0	0.30
Batticaloa	15.5	6.0	23.4	8.8	- 7.9	- 3.07
Badulla	59.9	10.1	89.8	14.4	- 30.0	- 4.86
Nuwara Eliya	74.0	17.1	105.3	22.7	- 31.3	- 6.92
Kegalle	93.0	14.5	140.1	20.2	- 46.9	- 7.19
Kalutara	99.0	13.6	137.5	18.2	- 38.6	- 7.34
Jaffna	25.7	3.7	88.4	11.6	- 62.7	- 8.90
Mannar	15.5	21.0	22.7	27.9	- 7.2	- 9.21
Kandy	148.3	12.8	264.0	20.7	-115.7	- 9.74
Galle	67.6	9.2	162.6	19.5	- 95.0	-12.88
Matara	56.6	9.7	176.2	25.0	-119.7	-20.34

(continued)

TABLE 1.6 (continued)

_____

Source: 1971 General Report, p. 52.

[a] Ordered highest positive to highest negative lifetime migration rate.

[b] Resident in the district in 1971 but born in another district.

[c] Born in the district but resident in another district in 1971.

[d] In thousands.

[e] In-migrants as a percentage of all Sri Lanka-born persons who were living in the district in 1971.

[f] Out-migrants as a percentage of all persons born in the district irrespective of district of residence in 1971.

[g] Net gain or loss divided by the number of persons born in Sri Lanka living in the district at the time of the census.

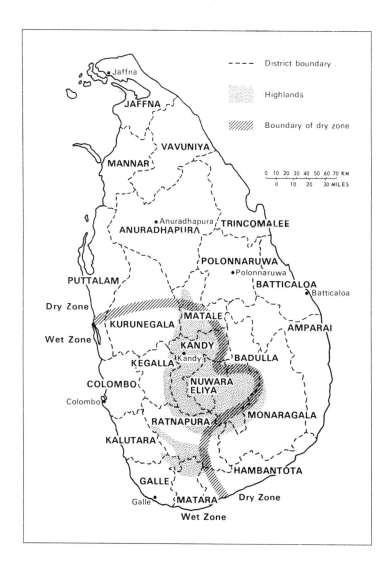

Figure 1.2   Sri Lanka, administrative districts at the time
of the 1971 census

and lifetime migration rate (r = -.40).[16] An important reservation is that urbanized Colombo district has continued to attract large numbers of in-migrants, although it has also contributed to the stream of out-migrants from the Southwest headed north and east.

High positive lifetime migration rates of 19 percent or higher were recorded for six districts, all in the north-central, northeastern, and southeastern Dry Zone. Matara and Galle in the densely populated south-coastal Wet Zone had the highest negative migration rates, followed by Kandy in the central highlands and Jaffna and Mannar in the far North.

Data on the districts of origin of the three largest streams of in-migration to each district (Table 1.7) and on the destinations of out-migrants from each district (Table 1.8) indicate a great deal of movement to adjacent districts and exchanges of persons between neighboring districts. The largest proportion of in-migrants to Kandy, for example, originated in Nuwara Eliya, while the largest proportion of in-migrants to Nuwara Eliya originated in Kandy. A similar exchange occurred between Galle and Matara. Trincomalee, in contrast, drew migrants from distant Jaffna, Nuwara Eliya, and Colombo. The attraction of Colombo is evident from the fact that it was among the three leading destinations for out-migrants from 18 districts. The generally northward flow of migrants was reversed in the far north, where Jaffna district sent migrants south to Vavuniya, Trincomalee, and Colombo.

SEX RATIOS AS CLUES TO MIGRATION

Features of internal migration in Sri Lanka may be illuminated further through detailed examination of district sex ratios.[17] Many of the materials relating to internal migration in Sri Lanka, as in other Asian countries, do not differentiate between male and female migration, presumably on the assumption either that the rates do not differ significantly or that gender differences in migration patterns are of little consequence. Our investigation of data relevant to migration within Sri Lanka suggests strongly that neither assumption is warranted. The use of sex ratios as indicators of migration, however, should be undertaken with caution. Sex ratios are at best only indirect measures of migration and by themselves leave many questions

TABLE 1.7

Districts of origin of the three largest streams of lifetime in-migrants, 1971

District of 1971 Residence[b]	District of Birth[a]					
	Largest		Second		Third	
Polonnaruwa	Kandy	(20.5)	Kegalle	(17.9)	Matale	(13.4)
Vavuniya	Jaffna	(44.3)	Kandy	(12.0)	Anuradhapura	(6.2)
Trincomalee	Jaffna	(17.3)	Nuwara Eliya	(14.9)	Colombo	(13.0)
Monaragala	Badulla	(47.6)	Hambantota	(9.8)	Matara	(9.7)
Anuradhapura	Colombo	(19.2)	Kandy	(18.9)	Kurunegala	(16.2)
Amparai	Kegalle	(13.6)	Matara	(12.3)	Kandy	(11.7)
Puttalam	Colombo	(48.1)	Kurunegala	(32.8)	Kalutara	(3.5)
Colombo	Galle	(15.8)	Kalutara	(13.8)	Matara	(12.5)
Hambantota	Matara	(66.3)	Galle	(8.6)	Monaragala	(4.4)
Kurunegala	Colombo	(33.5)	Kegalle	(15.2)	Puttalam	(15.0)
Ratnapura	Kalutara	(17.1)	Colombo	(16.2)	Matara	(15.3)
Matale	Kandy	(55.1)	Kurunegala	(11.2)	Colombo	(7.5)
Batticaloa	Jaffna	(21.6)	Colombo	(10.0)	Amparai	(9.8)
Badulla	Nuwara Eliya	(28.2)	Kandy	(23.3)	Colombo	(10.8)
Nuwara Eliya	Kandy	(55.1)	Badulla	(15.3)	Matale	(6.2)
Kegalle	Colombo	(30.9)	Kandy	(21.6)	Ratnapura	(15.2)
Kalutara	Colombo	(45.2)	Galle	(18.8)	Ratnapura	(8.8)

(continued)

19

TABLE 1.7 (continued)

District of 1971 Residence [b]	District of Birth [a]					
	Largest		Second		Third	
Jaffna	Kandy	(16.5)	Mannar	(15.9)	Colombo	(15.3)
Mannar	Jaffna	(42.3)	Colombo	(13.6)	Kandy	(8.0)
Kandy	Nuwara Eliya	(23.3)	Kegalle	(13.6)	Colombo	(13.2)
Galle	Matara	(30.8)	Kalutara	(24.6)	Colombo	(18.2)
Matara	Galle	(29.2)	Hambantota	(21.0)	Ratnapura	(14.9)

Source: 1971 General Report, p. 53.

[a] Figures in parentheses are the percentages of all lifetime in-migrants to the district of 1971 residence born in the district specified. For the numbers of in-migrants see Table 1.5.

[b] Ordered highest positive to highest negative lifetime migration rate.

TABLE 1.8

Districts of destination of the three largest streams of lifetime out-migrants, 1971

District[b] of Birth	District of 1971 Residence[a]		
	Largest	Second	Third
Polonnaruwa	Anuradhapura (17.3)	Colombo (13.1)	Kandy (9.7)
Vavuniya	Jaffna (28.5)	Anuradhapura (25.3)	Mannar (14.8)
Trincomalee	Amparai (26.9)	Colombo (17.4)	Anuradhapura (11.1)
Monaragala	Hambantota (21.2)	Amparai (20.6)	Badulla (19.6)
Anuradhapura	Colombo (19.2)	Kurunegala (14.9)	Kandy (10.0)
Amparai	Batticaloa (25.8)	Colombo (11.0)	Polonnaruwa (9.4)
Puttalam	Kurunegala (44.4)	Colombo (36.5)	Anuradhapura (4.1)
Colombo	Kurunegala (17.0)	Kalutara (16.0)	Puttalam (12.8)
Hambantota	Matara (30.4)	Ratnapura (23.2)	Colombo (15.2)
Kurunegala	Colombo (23.8)	Puttalam (20.5)	Anuradhapura (14.1)
Ratnapura	Colombo (30.3)	Kegalle (17.0)	Kalutara (10.4)
Matale	Kandy (28.0)	Anuradhapura (16.0)	Polonnaruwa (15.8)
Batticaloa	Trincomalee (29.8)	Amparai (16.1)	Colombo (11.1)
Badulla	Monaragala (27.4)	Colombo (17.4)	Nuwara Eliya (12.5)
Nuwara Eliya	Kandy (32.8)	Badulla (16.0)	Colombo (15.1)
Kegalle	Colombo (24.8)	Kurunegala (15.3)	Kandy (14.4)
Kalutara	Colombo (44.0)	Galle (12.1)	Ratnapura (11.4)

(continued)

TABLE 1.8 (continued)

District of Birth[b]	District of 1971 Residence[a]					
	Largest		Second		Third	
Jaffna	Colombo	(38.3)	Vavuniya	(16.5)	Trincomalee	(10.9)
Mannar	Colombo	(23.1)	Jaffna	(18.0)	Kandy	(8.0)
Kandy	Colombo	(20.0)	Nuwara Eliya	(15.4)	Matale	(14.0)
Galle	Colombo	(42.7)	Kalutara	(11.5)	Matara	(10.2)
Matara	Colombo	(31.1)	Hambantota	(19.8)	Galle	(11.8)

Source: 1971 General Report, p. 54.

[a] Figures in parentheses are the percentages of all lifetime out-migrants from the district of birth residing in 1971 in the district specified. For the numbers of out-migrants see Table 1.5.

[b] Ordered highest positive to highest negative lifetime migration rate.

unanswered. District sex ratios cannot alone provide information on numbers of migrants or rates of migration, but indicate only the "net" consequences of gender differentials in in- and out-migration. Furthermore, high (male preponderant) sex ratios can mean one of two things-- that males have migrated into an area, or that females have migrated out; low (female preponderant) sex ratios similarly can mean either that females have migrated in or that males have migrated out. Also, as indicated earlier, most districts are characterized by active streams of both in-migrants and out-migrants.

A deeper exploration of sex ratio imbalances by district and age group and their implications is undertaken in Chapter 2. Here we present only the broad picture of differentials by district, urban and rural areas, and ethnic communities.

Regional Differentials

In contrast to India, where the government has expressed concern over the ever-increasing masculinity of the nation's total sex ratio (all ages combined, urban and rural populations combined), in Sri Lanka the total sex ratio has been declining throughout the past century (Table 1.9). In 1871, the national sex ratio of Sri Lanka was 114.3, but in 1981 it was 103.1. Compared to the national sex ratios of other countries in Western Asia and South Asia, that of Sri Lanka appears quite balanced.[18]

A district-level view of 1981 sex ratios in Sri Lanka, however, reveals a great range of variation (Table 1.10). The sex ratios extend from a low of 93.8 in Matara district to a high of 129.8 in Polonnaruwa district. Taking 105.0 as the upper limit of what one could consider a "normal" sex ratio (that is, without cultural intervention), 10 out of 24 districts in 1981 had higher than normal sex ratios. There is a regional pattern, with the high sex ratios being found in the northern and eastern parts of the island, and also in Colombo in the southwest. Low sex ratios appear in the south-central region. It is generally thought that distortions in the overall sex ratio by district are the result of male-dominant interdistrict migration which displaces males from the densely populated Wet Zone to the relatively sparsely populated Dry Zone; these migrating males are then thought to be joined later by their wives. The male pioneer model seems supported by the data in

TABLE 1.9
National sex ratios at censuses of Sri
Lanka, 1871-1981

Census Year	Sex Ratio	Census Year	Sex Ratio
1871	114.3	1946	113.0
1881	113.9	1953	111.5
1891	112.7	1963	108.2
1901	113.5	1971	106.1
1911	112.6	1981	103.1
1921	112.5		

Source: For 1871-1971, General Report,
p. 73. For 1981, derived from Census,
1981, No. 1.

Table 1.11, which are aggregated at the national level and,
hence, do not indicate variations by district. The trend
toward lower sex ratios with longer durations in the
district is nonetheless apparent. Also, although not
evident from the data presented in Table 1.10, there is a
smaller but significant stream of female migrants into the
southern coastal districts, combining with an out-migration
of males to produce very low, female predominant, sex
ratios in these districts.

Growth Rates, Densities, and Sex Ratios

The close association of district population density,
population growth rate, and sex ratio can be depicted quite
vividly, as is indicated in Figure 1.3, which strongly
suggests the role of migration in skewing sex ratios.
(Urbanized Colombo and Gampaha districts are excluded due
to their very high population densities of, respectively,
about five and two times that of the next most densely
populated district. See Table 1.2.) The seven districts
with the lowest sex ratios, under 101, are all clustered in
the upper left corner of the figure, indicating high

TABLE 1.10
Sex ratios by district, 1946-1981

District[a]	1946	1953	1963	1971	1981[b] Total	Urban	Rural
Matara	99.9	101.7	98.5	97.5	93.8	95.3	93.6
Galle	97.6	96.6	97.0	97.7	93.9	98.3	92.8
Kegalle	112.9	109.5	106.3	103.8	97.8	107.5	97.1
Jaffna	99.8	100.4	101.1	99.5	98.1	100.6	96.9
Kalutara	105.7	105.0	102.7	101.5	98.2	100.5	97.5
Kandy	112.7	108.7	106.8	103.9	98.5	11?,0	96.6
Nuwara Eliya	110.2	109.8	106.4	104.1	100.3	123.9	98.6
Gampaha	---	---	---	---	101.2	104.5	100.0
Kurunegala	115.6	114.7	107.8	105.3	101.5	121.4	100.8
Badulla	111.5	112.1	107.0	104.5	102.0	111.5	101.2
Puttalam	118.5	116.1	108.1	106.0	102.0	105.1	101.6
Matale	114.7	115.4	108.0	106.3	102.4	108.9	101.7
Batticaloa	101.4	114.3	107.5	107.3	102.4	97.2	104.0
Hambantota	114.4	109.2	106.1	105.8	104.0	114.8	102.9
Ratnapura	118.1	114.8	110.6	108.9	106.5	113.6	106.0
Amparai	---	---	119.0	110.0	109.3	108.0	109.5
Colombo	121.7	117.9	113.0	110.1	110.6	113.6	102.2
Anuradhapura	144.0	135.4	119.3	115.3	113.4	127.0	112.4
Vavuniya	136.4	136.4	133.4	124.2	113.6	124.5	111.1
Mannar	147.3	145.1	121.1	116.4	114.1	112.0	114.4
Trincomalee	200.3	144.4	129.5	119.1	115.3	114.4	115.8
Monaragala	---	---	116.0	115.1	117.4	141.1	116.9
Mullaitivu	---	---	---	---	122.8	119.8	123.1
Polonnaruwa	---	---	136.7	124.9	129.8	142.4	128.8
Sri Lanka	113.0	111.5	108.2	105.8	103.1	109.1	101.6

(continued)

26

TABLE 1.10 (continued)

Source: For 1946-1971, Department of Census and Statistics, <u>Census of
Population, 1971</u>, Volume II, Part I (Colombo: Department of Government
Printing, 1975), p. 4 (hereafter cited as <u>Census, 1971</u>). For 1981,
derived from <u>Census, 1981</u>, No. 1.

a
Ordered lowest to highest sex ratio in 1981.

b
At the time of the 1981 Census, two new districts, Gampaha and
Mullaitivu, had been created. Additionally, other district boundaries
were redrawn. Affected districts include: Colombo, Kandy, Nuwara
Eliya, Mannar, Vavuniya, and Jaffna. Thus, figures for earlier years
for these districts are not strictly comparable to the 1981 figures.

TABLE 1.11
Sex ratios for interdistrict migrants by duration of stay in
district of 1971 residence

All Durations	Less Than 1 year	1-4 Years	5-9 Years	10 Years and Longer
111.0	135.2	122.2	108.9	98.2

Source: Derived from <u>1971 General Report</u>, p. 56.

population densities and low population growth rates. The
eight districts with the highest sex ratios, of 109 and
above, form a jagged line across the lower right portion of
the figure, indicating low population densities and very
high population growth rates. Between these two groups of
districts are sprawled seven districts with relatively
balanced (moderately masculine) sex ratios associated with
lower population densities than the districts in the former

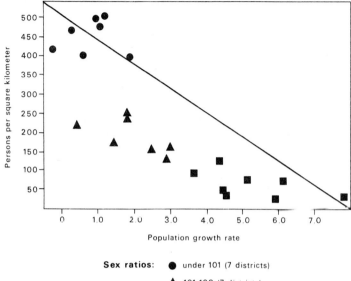

Figure 1.3   Districts by population density, 1981;
population growth rate, 1971-1981; and sex
ratio, 1981 (excluding Colombo and Gampaha
districts)

group and lower rates of population growth than the
districts in the latter group. The districts characterized
by high sex ratios, high population growth rates, and low
population densities lie in the north-central,
northeastern, and southeastern Dry Zone, while the
districts on the other end of the continuum on all three
variables are clustered in the southwestern Wet Zone except
for Jaffna at the island's northern tip (see Figure 1.4).

Rural-Urban Migration

Sri Lanka stands out among Asian countries as being
characterized by relatively low rates of urbanization.
Sex ratios indicate that migration to the major cities is
led by males, many of whom later leave the city or are
joined by females, as suggested in Table 1.12. Except for
the cities of Moratuwa and Galle, both situated in

28

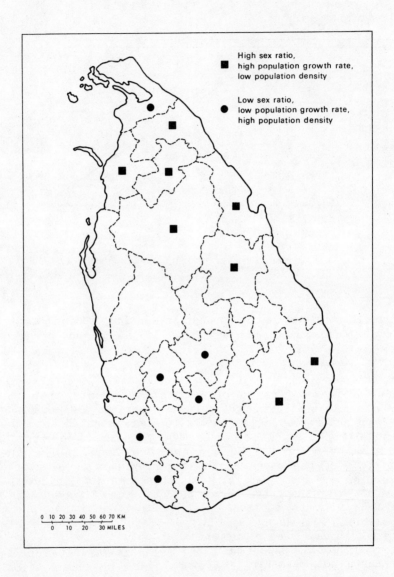

Figure 1.4   Locations of districts with highest and lowest
sex ratios depicted in Figure 1.3

TABLE 1.12

Sex ratios of migrants by duration of stay and of non-migrants, cities over 50,000 population, 1971

City	All Durations	Less Than 1 Year	1-4 Years	5-9 Years	10 Years and Longer	All Non-Migrants
Colombo	149.1	174.1	158.9	162.1	132.1	105.7
Dehiwala- Mt. Lavinia	112.0	113.5	115.6	108.2	101.7	108.8
Kotte	116.1	124.5	118.5	104.6	113.4	98.5
Moratuwa	95.6	115.8	95.6	100.1	78.0	97.4
Negombo	125.6	156.8	109.5	117.3	116.?	99.0
Kandy	115.8	146.3	126.7	105.7	100.2	105.6
Galle	94.6	116.7	104.6	81.8	83.9	102.5
Jaffna	124.6	151.8	145.0	121.7	109.3	100.7

Source: 1971 General Report, p. 63.

districts experiencing large net population losses through internal migration, the migrants of all durations in each city have higher (more masculine) sex ratios than the city's non-migrants (persons born and residing in 1971 in the municipal council area). Although there are some irregularities, the tendency in each case is for the sex ratio of the migrants to decline with duration of stay, so that the sex ratio at the longest duration is considerably lower than that of the shortest duration.

Ethnic Patterns

Sex ratios for the island's major ethnic communities, together with the communities' proportions of the total population, in 1946 and 1971 appear in Table 1.13. The sex ratios display little variation except for the "others" category, which, especially in 1946, included traders and merchants not permanently resident in Sri Lanka.[19] The

Table 1.13

Sex ratios and proportions of total population of major
ethnic communities, 1946 and 1971

	1946		1971	
Ethnic Community	Percent	Sex Ratio	Percent	Sex Ratio
Sinhalese	69.4	109.9	72.0	105.5
Sri Lanka Tamils	11.0	109.1	11.2	108.0
Indian Tamils	11.7	122.8	9.3	106.9
Sri Lanka Moors	5.6	112.7	6.5	106.4
Others	2.2	214.0	1.0	111.2

Source: Department of Census and Statistics, Census of
Ceylon, 1946, Vol. 1, part 2 (Colombo: Government Press,
1951), p. 105; Department of Census and Statistics,
Census of Population, 1971, Vol. 2, part 1 (Colombo:
Department of Government Printing, 1975), p. 25.

somewhat higher sex ratio of the Indian Tamils in 1946 may
reflect male migration from South India for employment
during the Second World War.[20] The near-uniformity of sex
ratios among ethnic communities in Sri Lanka stands in
marked contrast to the situation in North India, where
large caste groupings in the same region display different
sex ratios.[21] Sri Lankan ethnic group sex ratios may
reflect an underlying socio-cultural commonality, also
apparent in kinship and caste structures, despite
conspicuous differences of language and religion.

The overall similarity of the ethnic communities' sex
ratios suggests that regional variations in sex ratios are
not explicable in terms of the majority community of the
area. Table 1.14 presents sex ratios and proportions of
the population of the major communities by district in
1971. Districts with the highest and the lowest sex ratios
include both Sinhalese-majority and Sri Lanka Tamil-
majority areas. In districts in which the Sinhalese
constitute a majority of the population, the sex ratio for
the Sinhalese ranges from almost 125 in Polonnaruwa to

TABLE 1.14
Sex ratios and percentages of population of major ethnic communities, by district, 1971

District [a]	Sinhalese		Sri Lanka Tamils		Indian Tamils		Sri Lanka Moors	
	Percent	Sex Ratio	Percent	Sex Ratio	Percent	Sex Ratio	Percent	Sex Ratio
Polonnaruwa	89.8	124.9	3.0	133.1	0.2	204.5	6.9	119.6
Vavuniya	16.8	130.9	61.3	122.0	14.5	131.9	6.6	113.8
Trincomalee	29.1	132.8	35.2	114.3	2.7	146.0	31.7	110.6
Mannar	4.1	261.6	51.4	113.3	16.7	125.3	25.3	102.8
Anuradhapura	90.4	114.6	2.0	152.8	0.5	133.0	6.6	113.6
Monaragala	90.1	115.0	1.6	156.2	6.0	106.4	2.1	116.7
Colombo	83.1	107.4	6.3	135.3	2.2	151.1	5.5	112.7
Amparai	30.2	130.9	22.2	105.7	0.6	156.7	46.4	102.6
Ratnapura	88.8	109.0	1.4	132.5	17.1	105.4	1.2	123.4
Batticaloa	4.5	164.7	69.1	105.3	1.7	153.9	23.7	101.6
Matale	74.6	106.7	3.5	113.8	14.9	101.5	6.4	109.2
Puttalam	81.2	130.9	6.8	108.0	1.6	169.6	9.8	105.0
Hambantota	97.1	105.2	0.5	244.7	0.1	152.5	1.3	108.6
Kurunegala	92.8	104.6	0.9	142.7	1.3	115.5	4.5	110.0
Badulla	58.7	104.9	3.2	280.1	34.0	102.0	3.2	109.4
Nuwara Eliya	41.4	106.0	4.1	112.4	52.3	101.8	1.6	107.6

(continued)

TABLE 1.14 (continued)

District[a]	Sinhalese		Sri Lanka Tamils		Indian Tamils		Sri Lanka Moors	
	Percent	Sex Ratio	Percent	Sex Ratio	Percent	Sex Ratio	Percent	Sex Ratio
Kandy	62.3	103.6	4.3	118.0	24.1	103.0	8.2	101.3
Kegalle	84.0	103.3	1.7	123.4	9.4	105.0	4.4	103.5
Kalutara	86.6	101.0	1.0	135.8	5.3	106.1	6.9	100.0
Jaffna	1.0	243.5	94.9	97.5	2.6	135.5	1.4	122.9
Galle	94.3	97.2	0.5	145.4	2.1	108.9	3.0	100.0
Matara	93.9	97.1	0.3	152.9	3.2	105.8	2.5	96.0

Source: Department of Census and Statistics, Census of Population, 1971, Vol. 1, parts 1-22 (mimeographed; Colombo: Department of Census and Statistics, 1974), Table 9.

[a] Ordered highest to lowest district sex ratio.

about 97 in Matara. In Sri Lanka Tamil-majority districts, the highest and lowest sex ratios for that community are 122 in Vavuniya and 97.5 in Jaffna, virtually identical ranges for the two communities. In districts with high total sex ratios, all communities exhibit relatively high sex ratios with the exception of the Sri Lanka Moors (Muslims) in Mannar district. It appears that all major communities within a given district experience similar sex ratio imbalances.

Higher sex ratios characterize ethnic communities in districts in which that community is a small minority. In Galle and Matara districts, with total sex ratios of under 98 in 1971, the sex ratios for the small numbers of Sri Lanka Tamils were close to 150, and in Hambantota district, with a sex ratio of under 106, the ratio for the minute Sri Lanka Tamil minority was nearly 245. Similarly, in Jaffna district the sex ratio in 1971 was slightly below 100, but the tiny Sinhalese minority in the district had a sex ratio of more than 240. The supposition might be advanced that males migrating for work to districts in which their ethnic community is a small minority more frequently leave families behind than those migrating to districts in which their community constitutes the majority. Eruptions of communal violence such as occurred in 1977, 1981, and 1983, in which victims were generally the exposed and vulnerable members of one community residing among members of another community, may add a new and formidable constraint to family migration into districts in which their community is a minority.

CONCLUSION

Movements of population of considerable magnitude have characterized Sri Lanka over recent decades. Internal migration was stimulated by rapid population growth after 1945, and facilitated by government-sponsored irrigation projects and settlement schemes in the sparsely populated Dry Zone. The principal flow of migrants has been from the crowded Wet Zone to the lightly populated districts of the Dry Zone, producing in the latter districts very rapid rates of population growth. Some rural to urban migration has occurred, as is attested by the frequency with which Colombo district has appeared among the principal destinations of out-migrants from other districts. Nonetheless, most internal migration in Sri Lanka has been rural to rural. The general northeasterly flow of migrants has been reversed in the far North, where migrants from Jaffna have moved southward. Also, many districts have had sizable numbers of both in- and out-migrants and exchanges of persons between neighboring districts have been common.

Interdistrict migration frequently has involved male migrants journeying to Dry Zone destinations without their families, producing pronounced variations in sex ratios between districts. A smaller counter-stream of female migration into southern districts from which males are departing has created the often female-preponderant sex ratios in those districts. The role of migration in the skewing of sex ratios seems evident from the close association of sex ratios with district population growth rates and population densities. High sex ratios are found in the districts characterized by low population densities and very rapid rates of population growth, whereas low sex ratios and a preponderance of females in the population are found in the districts with high population densities and very low population growth rates. Male preponderance also has characterized rural to urban migration, although the sex ratios of migrants have declined with longer durations of urban residence, suggesting either that male migrants to the city return to the villages or that they are eventually joined by wives and families.

The major ethnic communities have displayed strikingly similar patterns of sex ratios. The socioeconomic and demographic character of the district seems to dictate a similar ratio between the sexes for members of all ethnic communities. An exception is provided by very small ethnic minorities in the district, which display heavily male sex ratios, presumably reflecting social and cultural obstacles to the movement of families to areas in which their ethnic community constitutes a very small minority. Further examination of imbalances in sex ratios and discussion of implications of marked sex ratio distortions appear in the following chapter.

NOTES

1.   Important studies of internal migration in developing countries include: Michael P. Todaro, <u>Internal Migration in Developing Countries: A Review of Theory, Evidence, Methodology and Research Priorities</u> (Geneva: International Labour Office, 1976); Alan Brown and Egon Neuberger, eds., <u>Internal Migration: A Comparative Perspective</u> (New York: Academic Press, 1977); Anthony H. Richmon and Daniel Kubat, <u>Internal Migration: The New World and the Third World</u> (Beverly Hills, CA: Sage Publications, 1976); John Connell, Biplab Dasgupta, Roy Laishley, and Michael Lipton, <u>Migration from Rural Areas: The Evidence from Village Studies</u> (Delhi: Oxford University Press, 1976); Calvin Goldscheider, ed., <u>Rural Migrants in Developing Nations: Comparative Studies of Korea, Sri Lanka, and Mali</u> (Boulder, CO: Westview Press, 1984); Calvin Goldscheider, ed., <u>Urban Migrants in Developing Nations: Patterns and Problems of Adjustment</u> (Boulder, CO: Westview Press, 1983). Compared to the literature on urban migration, the literature on rural-to-rural migration is quite sparse.

2.   For studies of internal migration in Sri Lanka see O.E.R. Abhayaratne and C.H.S. Jayewardene, "Internal Migration in Ceylon," <u>Ceylon Journal of Historical and Social Studies</u>, VIII, 1965, pp. 68-90; Dayalal Abeysekera, "Regional Patterns of Intercensal and Lifetime Migration in Sri Lanka," Papers of the East-West Population Institute, No. 75 (Honolulu, HI.: East-West Population Institute, 1981); United Nations, Economic and Social Commission for Asia and the Pacific, <u>Migration, Urbanization and Development in Sri Lanka</u> (New York: United Nations, Comparative Study on Migration, Urbanization and Development in the ESCAP Region, Country Report, ST/ESCAP/211, 1980); Shue Tuck Wong, "Net Migration and Agricultural Change in Sri Lanka," in R.B. Mandal, ed., <u>Frontiers in Migration Analysis</u> (New Delhi: Concept, 1981), pp. 439-454; Dayalal Abeysekera, "Rural to Rural Migration in Sri Lanka," in Calvin Goldscheider, ed., <u>Rural Migrants</u>, pp. 109-208; Robert N. Kearney and Barbara D. Miller, "Sex Differences in Patterns of Internal Migration in Sri Lanka," Women in International Development Working Paper Series No. 44 (East Lansing, MI: Michigan State University, Office of Women in International Development, 1984).

3. Department of Census and Statistics (Sri Lanka), Census of Population and Housing, Sri Lanka, 1981: Population Tables Based on a Ten Percent Sample, Preliminary Release No. 2 (Colombo: Department of Census and Statistics, 1982), Table 18. This publication is hereafter cited as Census, 1981, No. 2.

4. Department of Census and Statistics (Sri Lanka), Statistical Abstract of Sri Lanka [title varies] (Colombo: Department of Government Printing, annual).

5. Department of Census and Statistics (Sri Lanka), Census of Population, 1971, Sri Lanka: General Report (Colombo: Department of Census and Statistics, 1978), p. 18 (this volume is hereafter cited as 1971 General Report); Department of Census and Statistics (Sri Lanka), Census of Population and Housing, Sri Lanka, 1981, Preliminary Release No. 1 (Colombo: Department of Census and Statistics, 1981), p. 3 (this publication is hereafter cited as Census, 1981, No. 1).

6. Some of the recent and very illuminating work done on the social consequences of voluntary internal migration include: Colin Murray, Families Divided: The Impact of Migrant Labour in Lesotho (New York: Cambridge University Press, 1981); Leela Gulati, "Impacts of Male Migration to the Middle East on the Family: Some Evidence from Kerala," Working Paper No. 76 (Trivandrum, Kerala: Centre for Development Studies, 1983); and Judith Strauch, "Women in Rural-Urban Circulation Networks: Implications for Social Structural Change," in James T. Fawcett, Siew-Ean Khoo, and Peter C. Smith, eds., Women in the Cities of Asia: Migration and Urban Adaptation (Boulder, CO: Westview Press, 1984), pp. 60-77. Studies of forced relocation more often focus on the negative consequences of population movement; see, for example John Western, Outcast Cape Town (London: George Allen & Unwin, 1981); Robin Hallet, "Desolation on the Veld: Forced Removals in South Africa," African Affairs, LXXXIII, 1984, pp. 301-320; and Anastasia M. Shkilnyk, A Poison Stronger Than Love: The Destruction of an Ojibwa Community (New Haven, CT: Yale University Press, 1985).

7. See the discussions in: Jacqueline H. Straus and Murray A. Straus, "Suicide, Homicide, and Social Structure in Ceylon," Journal of Sociology, LVIII, March 1953, pp. 461-469; A.L. Wood, Crime and Aggression in Changing Ceylon, in Transactions of the American Philosophical Society, New Series, Vol. VI, Part 8 (Philadelphia: American

Philosophical Society, 1961); and Christopher M. Langford, "Fertility Change in Sri Lanka Since the War: An Analysis of the Experience of Different Districts," Population Studies, XXXV, 1981, pp. 285-306. The nineteenth-century introduction of meticulous British practices of record-keeping, a manageably small population, well-developed networks of transportation and communications, and high and rising literacy rates and educational levels all may be presumed to have contributed to the quality of the data. Census enumerations have been conducted in Sri Lanka since 1871, interrupted during the Great Depression and the Second World War, but resumed with censuses in 1946, 1953, 1963, 1971, and 1981.

8. Chilaw is included within Puttalam district, with which it was merged, in data reported here.

9. For a description of the climate and geography of Sri Lanka see Gerald Peiris, "The Physical Environment," in K.M. de Silva, ed., Sri Lanka: A Survey (Honolulu: University Press of Hawaii, 1977), pp. 3-30.

10. On the impact of population growth on agricultural holdings in an area of the central highlands see Cyril Paranavitana, "Land Hunger, Agrarian Changes and Government Policies: A Comparative Study of Nine Villages in Sri Lanka, 1955 & 1980," Marga (Colombo), VIII, 1985, pp. 22-39. Also, see H.G.D. Hemasiri, "Demographic Factors in Agricultural Development--Sri Lanka's Experience," Staff Studies, Central Bank of Ceylon, VII, September 1977, pp. 71-91; and, generally, Gavin W. Jones and S. Selvaratnam, Population Growth and Economic Development (Colombo: Hansa Publishers, 1972).

11. "A Survey of Employment, Unemployment and Underemployment in Ceylon," International Labour Review, LXXXVII, March 1963, p. 251; Department of Census and Statistics (Sri Lanka), Socio-Economic Survey of Sri Lanka, 1969-70, Rounds 1-4, Vol. I (Colombo: Department of Census and Statistics, 1973), pp. 32, 39.

12. See B.H. Farmer, Pioneer Peasant Colonization in Ceylon (London: Oxford University Press, 1957).

13. Central Bank of Ceylon, Department of Economic Research, Survey of Economic Conditions in the Mahaweli Development Area, 1974 (Colombo: Central Bank of Ceylon, 1975), p. 1; Central Bank of Ceylon, Annual Report of the Monetary Board to the Hon. Minister of Finance and Planning for the Year 1977 (Colombo: Central Bank of Ceylon, 1978), pp. 15-16.

14.   See K.H.W. Gaminiratne, "Some Aspects of Urbanization in Sri Lanka," Occasional Paper No. 3 (Colombo: Ministry of Information and Broadcasting and UNESCO/UNFPA, 1976).

15.   Department of Census and Statistics (Sri Lanka), Census of Ceylon, 1946, Vol. I, Part 1 (Colombo: Government Press, 1950), p. 74.

16.   Lifetime migration rate refers to net migration gain or loss as a proportion of the Sri Lanka-born district population.

17.   The term "sex ratio" refers to the number of males per one hundred females, following the standard practice throughout most of the world.

18.   An early article on the subject of comparative sex ratios noted the following 1961 national sex ratios: Pakistan, 112.7; India, 106.6; and Indonesia, 97.3.   See M.A. El-Badry, "Higher Female Than Male Mortality in Some Countries of South Asia: A Digest," Journal of the American Statistical Association, LXIV, December 1969, pp. 1234–1244.   Worldwide, nations with sex ratios above 105.0 are quite rare; they include India, Pakistan, and some countries in the Near East.

19.   Among those classified here as "others" in 1946 were Indian Moors, mostly traders, who had a sex ratio of 640.6.   Also in the "other" category were Burghers and Eurasians, Malays, and Veddahs, all of whom exhibited nearly balanced (near 100) sex ratios.   In 1971, a much smaller Indian Moor community, perhaps more permanently established in Sri Lanka, had a sex ratio of 137.0.   In that year, the sex ratio of the Burgher community was 98.0 and that of the Malays was 106.7.

20.   The very high sex ratio of 200.3 in Trincomalee district in 1946, presented in Table 1.10, presumably resulted from the temporary wartime employment of male workers, many from South India, at the Trincomalee naval base.

21.   Within districts, even villages, of India, different "caste" groups exhibit contrasting sex ratios with major differences between "upper castes" and "lower castes."   See Barbara D. Miller, The Endangered Sex: Neglect of Female Children in Rural North India (Ithaca, NY: Cornell University Press, 1981), chapter 4.

2

Unbalanced Sex Ratios

The very nature of migration, a move from a known and predictable environment to one that is unfamiliar, places stress on the migrant. Migrants to new areas exhibit a variety of coping responses which result in outcomes ranging from what could be termed successful integration into the new destination to maladapted behaviors such as depression and hypertension. Some recent research has sought to disentangle the determinants of varying patterns of adjustment. Factors examined include the presence or absence of kinship networks in the destination point, expectations regarding the new situation compared to what actually is encountered, employment patterns, the separation of spouses, and the degree of sociocultural difference between the migrants and the indigenous residents of the area.[1] One factor that has received little attention in the migration literature is the gender composition of migration streams.[2]

In this chapter we examine data on sex ratios as a key to possible causes of social and individual stress precipitated by voluntary internal migration in Sri Lanka. Migration which severely unbalances the sex ratio and keeps spouses divided for lengthy periods of time appears more likely to lead to social disruption than sex-balanced migration in which spouses and children migrate together or at least are not separated from each other for long. Balanced sex ratios are not necessarily always conducive to social harmony, but there is some research that clearly associates social disruption with highly male-preponderant sex ratios.[3] It is also known that some cultural situations seem adapted to the long-term migration of one spouse (usually the male), for example in trading communities of India such as the Marwaris.[4] While not taking unbalanced sex ratios and separated spouses as totally explanatory of some of the negative consequences of internal migration discussed in following chapters, we use the data to point to those districts, regions, and age groups in Sri Lanka in which the greatest potential stress might be anticipated.

Most of the analysis in this chapter is performed with 1971 district-level data (see Figure 1.2 for location of the districts), with some reference to 1981 data (Figure 1.1). We rely mainly on two kinds of information derived from the 1971 census: sex ratio data by district, and data on numbers of migrants by sex for eleven selected districts. In the former case, we can separate urban from rural, in the latter we cannot.

The chapter begins with a detailed review of sex ratios in various age groups by district. Next, for 11 districts, data are analyzed on numbers of male and female migrants in the population by age groups. The chapter concludes with a presentation of the relationship between certain sociocultural variables--employment, literacy, and age at marriage--and sex ratios, and a discussion of spouse separation as an important phenomenon related to highly unbalanced sex ratios in some parts of the island.

SEX RATIO VARIATIONS BY AGE GROUP

Juveniles

Sex ratios at birth in most national populations hover around 105.0.[5] Official statistics on sex ratios at birth in Sri Lanka by year from 1960 through 1979 indicate a range from a low of 103.1 to a high of 104.6 (Table 2.1). Thus in Sri Lanka the national sex ratio at birth is within the "normal" range.[6] Although we do not have district level data on sex ratios at birth, it is not likely that they could explain the district-by-district variation seen in Table 1.10.

The juvenile sex ratio (urban and rural combined) for all of Sri Lanka in 1971 was 103.0, within the range of normalcy (Table 2.2).[7] The variation among districts in the total juvenile sex ratio is slight: from a low of 100.6 in Vavuniya to a high of 104.8 in Trincomalee. Rural and urban juvenile sex ratios are also normal. Sri Lanka's juvenile sex ratios are similar to those found in districts

TABLE 2.1
Sex ratio at birth, 1960-1979 (live births)

Year	Sex Ratio	Year	Sex Ratio
1960	103.3	1970	104.0
1961	103.5	1971	104.4
1962	103.9	1972	104.3
1963	104.0	1973	104.6
1964	103.3	1974	103.6
1965	103.3	1975	103.0
1966	103.9	1976	104.0
1967	103.1	1977	103.7
1968	103.7	1978	104.5
1969	103.3	1979	104.1

Source: Department of Census and Statistics (Sri Lanka), Statistical Abstract of Sri Lanka [title varies] (Colombo: Department of Government Printing, annual), for 1977 and 1982.

TABLE 2.2
Sex ratios by district and 10-year age groups, 1971

District[a]	0-9	10-19	20-29	30-39	40-49	50-59	60-69	70 & Older
Colombo:								
Total	103.1	107.0	115.5	114.6	116.7	116.2	112.4	101.5
Urban	102.8	110.1	131.5	128.0	128.8	124.4	109.7	94.7
Rural	103.4	103.3	96.1	98.8	103.6	107.8	115.1	105.4
Kalutara:								
Total	103.1	101.7	94.9	96.4	104.3	108.8	110.9	107.0
Urban	103.3	102.8	100.3	101.4	108.2	105.7	102.9	90.9
Rural	103.1	101.4	93.5	95.0	103.2	109.7	113.2	112.1
Galle:								
Total	103.4	102.2	88.3	89.0	95.7	98.2	103.2	103.3
Urban	104.2	106.3	97.7	93.4	96.9	99.3	100.2	90.7
Rural	101.1	101.1	85.8	88.0	95.4	97.8	104.0	106.7
Matara:								
Total	103.3	100.4	85.2	90.2	97.4	98.0	109.1	104.2
Urban	101.4	100.4	97.8	94.6	101.6	94.9	98.6	96.7
Rural	103.5	100.5	83.6	89.6	96.9	98.5	110.7	105.4
Hambantota:								
Total	103.0	104.5	103.3	99.5	113.9	127.1	124.8	105.7
Urban	103.6	111.9	124.5	111.1	127.2	132.2	110.3	92.7
Rural	103.0	103.8	100.8	98.2	112.5	126.5	126.6	107.3
Ratnapura:								
Total	102.4	103.8	101.2	108.8	124.5	134.8	153.1	145.1
Urban	100.9	109.0	112.0	121.1	130.6	135.6	142.9	135.6
Rural	102.6	103.4	99.4	107.8	124.0	134.7	154.1	145.9
Kegalle:								
Total	103.3	101.3	91.0	98.9	113.0	124.9	139.1	127.9
Urban	98.5	106.0	106.6	113.6	132.2	125.8	137.8	123.5
Rural	103.7	101.0	89.9	97.8	111.6	124.8	139.2	128.2
Kandy:								
Total	103.7	101.3	93.3	101.4	113.3	119.3	135.1	125.6
Urban	105.5	116.2	125.3	120.2	131.8	131.6	133.9	116.8
Rural	103.5	99.2	89.1	98.8	110.8	117.7	135.2	125.2
Nuwara Eliya:								
Total	102.5	98.6	93.2	105.7	118.0	121.0	149.0	139.2
Urban	101.5	103.0	122.3	131.9	157.0	154.0	170.9	141.3
Rural	102.5	98.3	91.4	103.8	115.6	119.4	147.9	139.0
Matale:								
Total	102.6	100.6	97.6	102.9	121.9	136.4	145.6	139.2
Urban	103.2	103.5	107.9	109.7	132.2	139.8	145.2	187.8
Rural	102.5	100.2	96.2	102.0	120.5	136.0	145.7	140.6

TABLE 2.2 (continued)

District[a]	0-9	10-19	20-29	30-39	40-49	50-59	60-69	70 & Older
Monaragala:								
Total	103.3	105.7	111.7	123.9	156.7	172.3	173.1	161.6
Urban	104.1	112.1	138.4	162.4	175.3	223.8	187.5	137.8
Rural	103.3	105.5	110.9	122.8	156.2	170.9	172.6	162.4
Badulla:								
Total	102.5	100.6	93.1	105.6	121.7	123.1	140.1	129.4
Urban	101.2	107.0	117.9	122.4	137.2	141.0	138.2	121.3
Rural	102.6	100.0	90.0	104.0	120.2	121.4	140.3	130.2
Kurunegala:								
Total	102.8	102.7	96.2	97.7	113.7	128.2	149.0	129.3
Urban	103.5	112.9	137.7	124.2	146.5	150.5	160.8	134.1
Rural	102.8	102.3	94.4	96.5	112.3	127.3	148.6	129.2
Puttalam:								
Total	102.0	102.5	100.9	110.4	113.4	127.5	130.2	120.3
Urban	98.8	104.2	106.7	115.9	122.8	126.3	116.8	116.4
Rural	102.5	102.2	100.0	103.2	112.0	127.7	132.5	120.9
Anuradhapura:								
Total	102.9	107.2	115.9	117.7	142.3	166.7	180.4	163.7
Urban	103.0	115.5	162.1	146.7	158.0	167.4	169.0	131.9
Rural	102.9	106.3	110.6	114.3	140.4	166.6	181.7	167.6
Polonnaruwa:								
Total	100.7	115.3	139.2	136.8	171.6	185.3	192.4	197.0
Urban	98.1	167.3	284.9	203.6	266.7	266.7	185.7	205.3
Rural	100.9	111.2	124.5	130.3	166.3	179.0	193.0	196.2
Amparai:								
Total	102.6	103.9	109.5	121.5	131.9	136.9	122.9	100.6
Urban	101.5	98.8	101.3	111.1	126.9	114.6	104.0	66.2
Rural	102.7	104.6	110.6	123.1	132.6	140.4	126.1	107.4

(continued)

44

TABLE 2.2 (continued)

District[a]	0-9	10-19	20-29	30-39	40-49	50-59	60-69	70 & Older
Batticaloa:								
Total	102.5	102.4	105.3	107.8	126.6	137.5	114.0	114.3
Urban	101.9	105.7	106.1	107.4	115.0	124.6	110.1	98.1
Rural	102.7	101.2	105.0	107.9	131.4	143.3	115.7	121.8
Trincomalee:								
Total	104.8	108.2	120.7	137.5	150.9	170.6	157.5	148.6
Urban	106.7	108.5	120.7	139.5	160.4	173.3	122.3	113.3
Rural	103.7	108.0	120.7	136.2	145.1	168.8	185.2	184.1
Mannar:								
Total	102.6	101.0	118.0	131.7	145.8	176.8	159.2	143.9
Urban	104.1	110.1	113.7	134.4	132.0	133.5	168.2	128.4
Rural	102.4	99.6	119.0	131.2	148.3	185.5	157.5	146.6
Vavuniya:								
Total	100.6	115.0	133.2	137.7	158.8	201.2	188.8	159.5
Urban	99.4	114.6	143.7	153.1	172.8	183.5	182.0	151.7
Rural	100.8	115.1	129.9	133.2	154.9	207.0	190.9	161.6
Jaffna:								
Total	103.4	102.4	91.5	88.3	93.7	104.9	110.5	123.2
Urban	104.0	106.1	101.4	94.4	96.3	107.2	108.1	115.1
Rural	103.1	100.5	86.6	85.4	92.4	103.7	111.6	127.1
Sri Lanka:								
Total	103.0	103.4	101.1	104.8	114.6	120.4	125.5	116.4
Urban	102.9	108.9	122.4	119.8	123.9	122.5	113.0	101.1
Rural	103.0	102.0	94.9	100.5	111.9	119.7	129.3	120.9

Source: District data from which the sex ratios were derived were published as Table 6, Parts 1-22 of Department of Census and Statistics (Sri lanka), 1971 Census of Population, Vol. I (mimeographed; Colombo: Department of Census and Statistics, 1974), hereafter cited as Census, 1971, I. The Sri Lanka figures were derived from Department of Census and Statistics (Sri Lanka), Census of Population, 1971, Vol. II, Part 1 (Colombo: Department of Government Printing, 1975), pp. 13-15.

[a] Districts are ordered, beginning with Colombo, then moving from the southwest to the north and northeast of the island.

of neighboring South India, especially in the state of Kerala. They correspond to what census data on mortality in the juvenile years indicate: in 1970-1972, the age-specific death rate in the 1-4 age-group was 5.39 for boys and 6.37 for girls, and in the 5-9 age-group 1.68 for boys and 1.81 for girls.[8] These balanced sex ratios are a good indicator that sex differentials in childhood mortality are not significant in Sri Lanka, as they are in other regions of South Asia.[9]

10-19 Year-Olds

The amount of individual migration below the age of 10 years in Sri Lanka is probably negligible, but between the ages of 10 to 19, inter-district migration becomes important. Among the 10-19 year-olds, overall sex ratios (urban and rural combined) extend from a low of 98.6 in Nuwara Eliya to a high of 115.3 in Vavuniya. Urban sex ratios are lowest at 98.8 in Amparai and highest at 167.3 in Polonnaruwa. Very high rural sex ratios for the young adult population are not common, with only Vavuniya and Polonnaruwa in the northeast having rural sex ratios above 110. Districts in which rural sex ratios were more feminine in the 10-19 year age-group than in the previous category are found in the center and west of the island. The five most urbanized districts--Colombo, Jaffna, Kandy, Kalutara, and Galle--all have fewer males per females in this age category than in the younger group, but the difference is often slight.

Most urban sex ratios in the 10-19 year age category fall between 98.8 (Amparai) and 116.2 (Kandy); Polonnaruwa stands alone with a sex ratio of 167.3. Extreme urban masculinity, such as is characteristic of certain African cities where males may outnumber females two to one,[10] is not generally found in Sri Lanka, although in the upper age groups masculinity rises to a very high level. Polonnaruwa's urban population is, again, the extreme case, but its urban population is very small.

20-29 Year-Olds

In the central and western districts again, the 20-29 age group has fewer rural males per females than in the previous age group. The difference is most notable in

Galle and in the northern district of Jaffna. In contrast, there are several districts with higher rural sex ratios in this age group than in the previous group; highest sex ratios are found in Polonnaruwa, Trincomalee, and Vavuniya. This extreme masculinization corresponds with expectations produced by the male pioneer model (discussed in Chapter 1). Since the mean age at marriage for females in Sri Lanka in 1971 was 23.5 years,[11] we would not expect associational migration of females to occur until they had reached their late twenties and early thirties.

In this age-group, urban sex ratios are generally male-preponderant with only Galle and Matara on the southern coast having more urban females than males. The highest urban sex ratios are in northeastern towns.

Older Adults

If the male pioneer model were fully actuated, sex ratios in the northeast should be fairly balanced in the 30-39 age-group, with husbands and wives at last united in the migration destination. In fact, the great majority of districts excepting only Hambantota and Jaffna, have fewer females per males in this age category than in the previous one. The highest rural sex ratios are found in Trincomalee, Vavuniya, Mannar, and Polonnaruwa. Colombo, Kandy, and Matale have fairly balanced sex ratios. Those with the lowest sex ratios are Galle, Matara, and Jaffna.

Urban sex ratios in this age group are at variance with those of the previous age group. In some districts, such as Polonnaruwa, Anuradhapura, and Jaffna, sex ratios are lower than in the previous group, which could indicate wives joining husbands for residence in the cities, or a return migration of males from the cities to the rural areas. These processes are similar to what could be hypothesized for larger cities (Table 1.12). Conversely, in other districts--Monaragala, Mannar, and Nuwara Eliya-- the urban sex ratio is more masculine in this age group than in the previous group. The tendency is for these latter districts to exhibit even higher sex ratios in older age categories, a phenomenon difficult to explain either on the basis of common sense or the census data.

In Colombo, Kalutara, Galle, Matara, and Jaffna, sex ratios for adults aged 40 years and older are fairly balanced; all other districts have extremely high levels of both rural and urban masculinity. Urban sex ratios go as high as 228.6 in Polonnaruwa, but, since numbers in the older categories are very small, we shall not emphasize the sex ratios in the older population and will merely note that they are all male-preponderant.

Summary of the Sex Ratio Data

Districts in the more urbanized and densely populated Wet Zone experience a deficit in rural males in the ages from 10 to 30 years, but up to the fifties in Galle. This pattern contrasts with that of the districts in the Dry Zone, especially those most affected by government colonization schemes--Amparai, Vavuniya, and Polonnaruwara--where there is never a preponderance of females and rarely a balanced sex ratio among any age group except that of juveniles.

DATA ON MIGRANTS IN THE POPULATION

The 1971 population census provides direct migration data on persons resident in a district but not born in the district, but unfortunately these data are not disaggregated by urban and rural sectors. While not strictly comparable to the above data on sex ratios due to the combination of urban and rural populations and the different age categories provided, these data do supply important complementary information. We obtained data on migrants in the population by sex and age for 11 districts. They are the five districts with the highest positive and the five with the highest negative lifetime migration rates, plus Colombo (Table 2.3). The 11 districts represent a good sample for the entire nation since some are more urbanized, and some are the sparsely populated colonization districts.

The numbers of males and females in various age groups not born in the district where they resided in 1971 are presented in Table 2.3 and displayed graphically for Colombo, Galle, and Polonnaruwa in Figure 2.1. On the basis of general knowledge of Sri Lankan migration patterns and sex ratio data, one would expect to see preponderantly male in-migration in Anuradhapura, Polonnaruwa, and Vavuniya. In these districts male in-migrants consistently outnumber female in-migrants at all age categories, except in the very oldest group in Polonnaruwa. The disparity is marked in all adult categories, requiring a rethinking of

48

TABLE 2.3
District population not born in the district, by sex and age, 11 selected districts, 1971[a]

District[b]	0-14	15-24	25-34	35-44	45-64	65 and Older
Colombo						
Males	80,341 (16.7)	100,203 (34.0)	91,646 (45.1)	70,227 (46.5)	82,083 (41.9)	21,067 (33.3)
Females	76,651 (16.6)	85,186 (31.8)	82,216 (45.6)	67,174 (49.0)	75,417 (43.3)	24,417 (39.6)
Sex Ratio	104.8	117.6	111.5	104.5	108.8	86.3
Galle						
Males	15,370 (16.7)	11,525 (16.7)	9,810 (22.5)	10,169 (28.0)	13,114 (26.0)	5,288 (23.5)
Females	14,470 (10.6)	14,030 (18.7)	15,626 (30.5)	14,741 (35.4)	16,688 (32.3)	7,119 (30.9)
Sex Ratio	106.2	82.1	62.8	70.0	78.6	74.3
Matara						
Males	13,627 (12.4)	8,614 (17.1)	8,130 (26.8)	8,437 (34.4)	10,844 (30.2)	3,916 (23.1)
Females	13,030 (12.3)	11,378 (19.1)	12,815 (36.0)	11,849 (40.0)	12,913 (36.1)	4,529 (28.9)
Sex Ratio	104.6	75.7	63.4	71.2	84.0	86.5

TABLE 2.3 (continued)

District[b]	0-14	15-24	25-34	35-44	45-64	65 and Older
Kandy						
Males	27,038 (11.5)	28,348 (23.6)	26,698 (33.9)	25,656 (41.1)	36,667 (46.4)	9,996 (39.6)
Females	25,816 (11.3)	34,347 (26.8)	38,675 (46.1)	29,166 (50.1)	34,333 (50.5)	8,316 (42.9)
Sex Ratio	104.7	82.5	69.0	88.0	106.8	120.2
Monaragala						
Males	7,032 (15.8)	6,804 (39.6)	6,511 (57.5)	5,635 (53.3)	5,393 (57.3)	1,632 (55.1)
Females	6,285 (14.4)	6,168 (36.7)	5,882 (57.0)	3,839 (49.3)	3,038 (50.2)	843 (49.8)
Sex Ratio	111.9	110.3	110.7	146.8	177.6	196.3
Anuradhapura						
Males	12,616 (14.0)	14,231 (34.3)	11,766 (52.4)	10,421 (53.2)	12,433 (51.5)	3,198 (44.1)
Females	11,788 (13.7)	12,297 (30.6)	10,357 (50.4)	8,777 (50.2)	7,942 (51.1)	1,672 (38.2)
Sex Ratio	107.0	115.7	113.6	118.7	157.9	191.3
Polonnaruwa						
Males	6,299 (16.6)	9,832 (55.1)	10,103 (81.7)	7,357 (83.2)	7,729 (85.0)	1,864 (83.0)
Females	6,083 (16.5)	7,423 (47.9)	7,161 (77.7)	5,435 (80.9)	4,542 (82.5)	1,083 (83.8)
Sex Ratio	103.6	132.5	141.1	135.4	170.2	172.1
Trincomalee						
Males	5,252 (12.9)	7,754 (44.0)	7,059 (58.3)	5,805 (60.1)	6,456 (64.7)	1,247 (51.5)
Females	4,770 (8.0)	5,653 (35.5)	5,165 (51.0)	3,374 (52.5)	3,523 (54.0)	871 (44.1)
Sex Ratio	110.1	137.2	136.7	172.1	183.3	143.2

(continued)

TABLE 2.3 (continued)

District[b]	0-14	15-24	25-34	35-44	45-64	65 and Older
Mannar						
Males	1,652 (10.3)	2,525 (31.9)	2,304 (51.6)	2,084 (51.8)	2,350 (47.7)	563 (37.0)
Females	1,697 (10.7)	1,469 (22.2)	1,441 (37.7)	1,253 (38.2)	1,118 (33.0)	283 (27.2)
Sex Ratio	97.3	171.9	159.9	166.3	210.2	198.9
Vavuniya						
Males	3,429 (18.0)	4,612 (46.7)	3,870 (63.2)	3,216 (66.2)	4,235 (64.5)	765 (50.0)
Females	3,079 (15.9)	3,597 (42.4)	2,981 (60.1)	2,063 (57.4)	2,125 (59.9)	465 (47.3)
Sex Ratio	111.4	128.2	129.8	155.9	199.3	164.5
Jaffna						
Males	6,056 (4.9)	7,681 (12.3)	6,832 (20.4)	4,439 (15.7)	7,690 (16.6)	2,336 (11.7)
Females	5,933 (4.9)	6,495 (9.7)	6,495 (16.2)	4,737 (13.9)	4,925 (10.6)	1,459 (8.6)
Sex Ratio	102.1	118.3	105.2	93.7	156.1	160.3

Source: Derived from Census, 1971, I, Parts 1, 3, 6, 7, 9, 10, 11, 14, 17, 18, and 20.

[a] Numbers in parentheses are the percentage of total district population in that age and sex group not born in the district.

[b] Districts are ordered regionally as in Table 2.2.

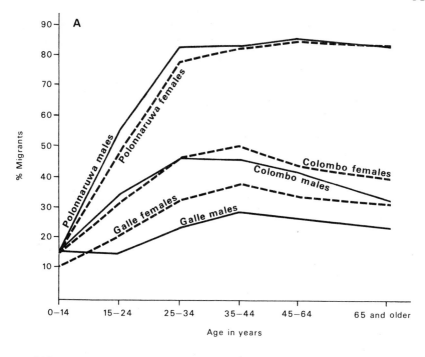

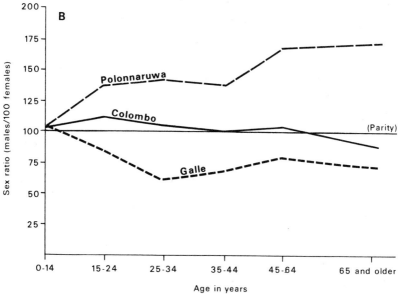

Figure 2.1 Colombo, Galle, and Polonnaruwa districts, A:
migrants as a percentage of age groups by sex,
and B: sex ratios of migrants by age groups

the male pioneer model which assumes the eventual union of husband and wife. Does this mean that male in-migrants marry local women? Or do the male in-migrants leave their wives behind throughout the course of the marriage and return occasionally for visits, as is common in many parts of the world? Both possibilities are quite likely and there is some documentation in the ethnographic literature on Sri Lanka for the former.[12]

Colombo has a unique configuration among the 11 districts. Male in-migrants are more numerous in the young adult years, with fairly balanced numbers of males and females in the ages 35-64 years, and a preponderance of females in the oldest age-group.

Kandy, Matara, and Galle have similar sex ratios except in the case of Kandy's oldest age groups which are male-preponderant. In all three districts, female in-migrants outnumber male in-migrants throughout most of the adult age groups. The predominantly female character of migration into Galle district is evident in Figure 2.1, which clearly depicts the higher proportion of in-migrants within the female than within the male population of the district in all adult age groups. Previous writing on internal migration in Sri Lanka has emphasized male migration and overlooked female migration, particularly the female-dominant stream to the Wet Zone districts of the south coast. This female-dominant stream constitutes only about 6 percent of district populations, compared to migrants constituting 20 and 30 percent of the female populations of some Dry Zone districts, but in which male migrants constitute an even larger proportion of the male population. At this point, we are not able to state why females predominate in the migration streams to the southern Wet Zone districts. One hypothesis is that employment in the coir industry attracts women to the region.[13]

On the basis of the data on numbers of migrants by sex for these 11 districts, three major patterns of internal migration in Sri Lanka can be distinguished. The first pattern, manifest in Colombo district (urban and rural combined), is relatively sex-egalitarian, though males lead in the early years. The second pattern is heavily male-preponderant and involves males migrating into the less densely populated districts of the Dry Zone. The third pattern is female-preponderant migration and is focused on districts in the Wet Zone. The first pattern conforms to general expectations: male migrants, some accompanied and others joined later by wives, which results in a fairly balanced sex ratio in the older age groups. The second pattern conforms only partly to the male pioneer model: numerous males do indeed migrate to the Dry Zone, but a balanced number of males and females is never attained. The third pattern demonstrates the existence of autonomous female migration, a stream not as numerically significant as the second pattern, but nonetheless important.

SOCIOCULTURAL CORRELATES

The 1971 census provides district data on several important sociocultural measures including employment, literacy, and age at marriage. Having delineated three patterns of migration associated with certain districts, we can now ask if these districts exhibit characteristic configurations for these sociocultural variables. Is employment higher or lower in male-preponderant districts? Are literacy rates associated with heavy male in-migration or female in-migration? Does age at marriage appear to have any relationship with gender-differentiated migration streams to various districts? The 1971 district data on employment by sex, literacy by sex, and age at marriage for females (data are not available for age at marriage for males by district) are presented in Table 2.4. Correlation coefficients between these variables and sex ratios are displayed in Table 2.5. The purpose of examining these variables is not to seek their possible causal influences on migration, but to reveal some of the important social characteristics of the district populations with differing types of internal migration patterns.

Male labor participation rates range from a low of 64.2 percent in Matara district to a high of 76.0 percent in Mannar district, thus displaying a much narrower differential than female labor participation rates. Female labor participation rates exhibit a wide range of variation, extending from a low of 5.3 percent in Mannar district to a high of 53.1 percent in Nuwara Eliya (Table 2.4).[14] High female labor participation rates in Nuwara Eliya, Badulla, and Kandy are largely attributable to the employment of women pluckers on tea estates. In Kandy district, for example, 68.7 percent of all employed women in 1971 were classified as tea pluckers and tea estate laborers.[15] The lowest female labor participation rates are found in the districts of Mannar, Batticaloa, Jaffna,

TABLE 2.4
Labor participation rate, literacy rate, and singulate mean age at
marriage, Sri Lanka, 1971

District[a]	Rate of Labor Participation[b]		Literacy[c]		Female Age at Marriage[d]
	Females	Males	Females	Males	
Nuwara Eliya	53.1	70.8	48.3	78.9	23.4
Badulla	39.3	67.5	51.5	78.2	23.3
Kandy	35.0	67.0	63.9	84.2	24.0
Ratnapura	33.7	70.0	61.0	81.1	23.8
Anuradhapura	32.8	71.4	66.2	84.2	21.4
Matale	29.9	68.6	63.3	82.7	22.7
Galle	29.6	65.9	77.2	88.1	25.8
Kalutara	27.5	67.9	77.7	88.6	25.2
Matara	26.8	64.2	71.4	85.6	25.7
Kegalle	26.3	65.7	70.3	86.2	24.4
Kurunegala	24.9	67.9	74.0	88.0	22.8
Colombo	23.0	69.2	84.4	91.9	24.4
Monaragala	20.7	70.5	52.8	75.2	21.0
Puttalam	20.7	72.4	79.1	88.0	22.1
Polonnaruwa	18.1	74.5	69.6	84.2	21.0
Hambantota	17.8	66.9	63.9	82.7	23.5
Vavuniya	10.1	75.3	69.9	81.8	20.3
Amparai	8.4	72.4	50.7	76.4	20.1
Trincomalee	8.1	72.7	57.6	76.4	19.7
Jaffna	7.8	64.6	79.2	86.3	23.4
Batticaloa	6.6	72.3	46.7	66.4	20.1
Mannar	5.3	76.0	68.0	82.4	20.2
Sri Lanka	26.0	68.4	70.9	86.5	23.5

Source: For labor participation rates, 1971 General Report, pp.
127-128; for literacy, 1971 General Report, p. 116; for age at
marriage, Department of Census and Statistics, The Population of Sri
Lanka, p. 41.

TABLE 2.4 (continued)

---

[a] Ordered by female labor participation rate, from highest to lowest.

[b] The labor participation rate, referred to in the census report as activity rate, is the percentage of the population aged ten years and older who are in the labor force, i.e., "who contribute to the supply of labour for the production of economic goods and services," including persons currently unemployed but available for employment (1971 General Report, p. 123).

[c] The literacy rate is the percentage of persons ten years of age and older who "could read and write, with understanding, a short statement on everyday life in at least one language" (1971 General Report, p. 111).

[d] See footnote 11.

TABLE 2.5
Simple correlation coefficients between district
sex ratios and sociocultural variables, 1971

Sociocultural Variables	Sex Ratio
Female Labor Participation Rate	-.40*
Male Labor Participation Rate	.84**
Female Literacy Rate	.27
Male Literacy Rate	-.36*
Mean Age at Marriage of Females	-.82**

Source: Computed by the authors.

* Significant at less than the .05 level.
** Significant at less than the .01 level.
Non-starred items are not significant at less than the .1 level.

and Trincomalee, where the Sri Lanka Tamil ethnic community predominates with its presumably strong cultural restrictions against women's employment.[16] In fact, the presence of Sri Lanka Tamils in the population is strongly and negatively correlated with female labor participation rate (r = -.69). Mannar, Batticaloa, and Trincomalee districts also contain relatively large numbers of Sri Lanka Moors.

A simple correlation between male participation rates and sex ratios, and female participation rates and sex ratios reveals that in both cases there is a significant relationship. Male labor participation rates are strongly and positively correlated with sex ratios (Table 2.5). That is, where males are preponderant in the migration stream, then males have a higher participation rate. Conversely, female labor participation rates are strongly and negatively related to sex ratios. In other words, where the sex ratio is high (i.e., migration is male-preponderant), female participation rates are low.

The Dry Zone does not offer as many employment opportunities for women as are found in the Wet Zone.[17] In the Wet Zone work opportunities exist for women in the rubber and coconut industries. Also, there seems less availability of employment for women in small factories and in other non-agricultural occupations in the Dry Zone, relative to the Wet Zone. A study comparing women's work options in Kalutara district in the southwest to those in the Mahaweli region of Anuradhapura district documents this contrast.[18] One might hypothesize that women would have higher participation rates where in-migration has had a longer history and irrigated agriculture and non-agricultural opportunities have developed than they would have in more recently settled districts. But such is not clearly so: in comparing Amparai district (older settlements) to Polonnaruwa district (more recent settlements), we find lower female labor participation in Amparai. Interestingly, quite high female labor participation is found in Anuradhapura. Clearly, no simple explanation is revealed in the data.

Classic internal migration theory states that literacy has a positive effect on internal migration rates. In Sri Lanka, both the male and female populations are highly literate compared to other developing countries. Male literacy ranges from a low of 66.4 percent in Batticaloa district to a high of 91.9 percent in Colombo (Table 2.4). Female literacy ranges from a low of 46.7 percent in

Batticaloa to a high of 84.4 percent in Colombo. Literacy rates for males and females are strongly and positively correlated with each other (r = .91). Female literacy is not significantly correlated with sex ratio, while male literacy correlates moderately and negatively with sex ratio (r = -.36), thus implying that in districts of heavy male in-migration, males are less literate than elsewhere (Table 2.5). We are not able to say whether this finding stems from the lower literacy rates of migrants or of non-migrants in those districts, or a combination of both circumstances.

Thus, Sri Lanka stands apart from other Asian countries in which literacy appears in close relationship with the level of internal migration for females.[19] It must be remembered, however, that Sri Lanka stands out also as having one of the most literate populations of all the developing countries of Asia.

In Sri Lanka, the mean age at marriage for females ranges from a low of 19.7 years in Trincomalee district to a high of 25.8 years in Galle (Table 2.4). There is a clear regional pattern of lower age at marriage in the northeast and later age at marriage in the southwest.[20] Age at marriage for females is strongly and negatively correlated with sex ratio (r = -.82). Additionally, age at marriage of females is strongly and positively correlated with female labor participation (r = .59), and moderately strongly with female literacy (r = .47).

Areas of male out-migration and female in-migration such as Galle and Kalutara in the southwest are characterized by late age at marriage for females and high female labor participation rates. Areas of preponderantly male in-migration exhibit early marriage age for females and low labor participation of females.

Spouse Separation

These factors connect very tellingly with some apparent sociocultural sequelae of heavy male in-migration in the settlement areas of the northeast. These consequences are largely the result of the separation of nuclear and sub-nuclear units from the extended family context and, more generally, displacement of persons from villages where ties between nuclear units are strong and extensive to villages composed of unrelated nuclear or sub-nuclear units.

Census data show that in Sri Lanka many spouses live in separation from one another. Although distances between most areas of the island can be traversed in a day's journey by bus, which facilitates occasional visiting, the fact remains that for many couples family ties are stretched over space. Examination of the spouse separation rate for a small number of districts shows that only in Galle and Kalutara (districts of female in-migration) are there urban areas with large numbers of married women living without husbands, while rural areas of many districts are characterized by wives living without husbands (Table 2.6). In the settlement districts, as

TABLE 2.6
Spouse separation rates for selected
districts, 1971[a]

District	Urban	Rural
Colombo	6.1	- 8.2
Galle	-8.2	-11.3
Kalutara	-4.4	- 6.9
Kandy	8.1	- 5.8
Nuwara Eliya	9.3	- 2.1
Matale	2.4	2.1
Anuradhapura	14.6	4.8
Polonnaruwa	28.3	6.6

Source: Census, 1971, I, Parts 1-6, 17-18.

[a] The rate was calculated by taking the number of married males minus the number of married females as a percentage of the married males, following Sopher, note 18. Positive numbers indicate a preponderance of husbands living without wives, while negative numbers indicate wives living separate from husbands. "Marriage" includes both registered and customary unions.

expected, there are numerous husbands living without wives in both the urban and rural areas, although the rate of spouse separation is much higher in the towns in those districts.

CONCLUSION

The possibility is strong that extremely male-preponderant sex ratios may precipitate social disruption and be a factor contributing to less than optimal adjustment of migrants in the destination area. Nevertheless, such a relationship cannot be proven at this time for Sri Lanka. The data reviewed above on regional and age-group variations in sex ratios only allow a conjectural formulation of those places and ages at which social and psychological problems might be most likely to occur.

The sex ratio data and data on migrants in the population both point to several important facts about gender-differentiated migration in Sri Lanka that should be borne in mind. First, the generally held conception of the male pioneer migrant later joined by his wife does not hold true for most of the migraiton to the Dry Zone in the northeast. This large stream of rural-to-rural migrants is heavily male in all age groups. Second, there is a smaller but still measurable stream of female migrants to the Wet Zone in the southwest. The stream results in a preponderance of females in those districts in most age groups, but the sex ratio imbalance is not nearly as extreme as in the case of the male-preponderant Dry Zone. Third, although one might expect the large migrant stream toward Colombo to be extremely male-preponderant, such is not the case. Urban sex ratios are extremely masculine (in the 150-200 range) in the Dry Zone, moderately masculine (in the 120-130 range) in Colombo, and balanced (in the 95-105 range) in towns and cities of the Wet Zone.

In the districts where masculinity in sex ratios is extremely high, the imbalance begins with age group 20-29 years and generally continues through all older groups. These districts are in the Dry Zone. In the Wet Zone, by way of contrast, the tendency is for sex ratios to be somewhat more feminine in the age groups 20-29 and 30-39 but the variation between these groups and both younger and older groups is only about five or ten points compared to differences of 50 and 100 points in Dry Zone districts.

The numbers of migrants in the population, based on the sample of 11 districts, indicate that again in the Dry Zone districts--especially Anuradhapura, Polonnaruwa, and Vavuniya--both male and female migrants constitute half or more of the population in the age groups 25-34 years, 35-44 years, and 45-64 years. In the Wet Zone districts of Galle and Matara, male and female migrants constitute only about one-fourth or one-third of the population in the same age groups.

The data on selected sociocultural variables indicate that in the Dry Zone districts there is high male labor participation and low female labor participation, a contrast to the situation in the Wet Zone districts where male labor participation is low and female labor participation high. Spouse separation rates for eight districts show that the rate of husbands without wives is high in the Dry Zone districts of Anuradhapura and Polonnaruwa while the rate of wives without husbands is high in the Wet Zone districts of Galle and Kalutara, as well as in rural areas of Colombo and Kandy. It must be remembered, however, that the numbers of separated males in the Dry Zone districts are much larger than the numbers of separated females in the Wet Zone districts.

Thus, in terms of unbalanced sex ratios and sheer numbers of migrants, the prime adult age groups in the Dry Zone appear to be a population that might be at much greater risk of social and psychological problems than migrant populations in other districts. The sociocultural data likewise point to the Dry Zone as an especially volatile area.

NOTES

1. An excellent discussion of many of these issues is provided in Alden Speare, Jr., "Methodological Issues in the Study of Migrant Adjustment," in Calvin Goldscheider, ed., Urban Migrants in Developing Nations: Patterns and Problems of Adjustment (Boulder, CO: Westview Press, 1983), pp. 21-42; and four case studies included in the volume document the importance of many of these variables in affecting migrant adjustment. The case studies in the volume all concern rural-to-urban migration.

2. A recent and notable exception to this

generalization for Asia is James T. Fawcett, Siew-Ean Khoo, and Peter C. Smith, eds., Women in the Cities of Asia: Migration and Urban Adaptation (Boulder, CO: Westview Press, 1984).

3. A review of evidence from more than 500 tribal societies found a strong correlation between male-preponderant sex ratios among youths and the propensity for warfare; see William Divale and Marvin Harris, "Population, Warfare, and the Male Supremacist Complex," American Anthropologist, LXXVIII, 1976, pp. 521-538.

4. Hanna Papanek has drawn attention to the "separate worlds" of men and women among the Memon, a Muslim trading group of the Pakistan Punjab in "Men, Women and Work: A Comparison of Separate Worlds in Muslim South Asia and Two-Person Careers in America," Occasional Paper Series, Muslim Studies Sub-Committee of the Committee on Southern Asian Studies (Chicago, IL: University of Chicago, 1972). There is scattered, and highly varied, evidence concerning the effect of semi-permanent migration of males on the females who remain behind. In some instances, women's position seems strengthened, most notably as in the case of the matrilineal Nayars among whom men were traditionally absent for long periods of warfare. In other instances, the women who remain behind accrue double workloads, especially in agricultural contexts where male labor is scarce; a prime example of this situation is found in Himachal Pradesh, where many males migrate to the plains for work or to join the army and the women inherit all the farm work.

5. Barbara D. Miller, The Endangered Sex: Neglect of Female Children in Rural North India (Ithaca, NY: Cornell University Press, 1981), pp. 38-39, 171-173; Samuel H. Preston, Mortality Patterns in National Populations--With Special Reference to Recorded Causes of Death (New York: Academic Press, 1976); Pravin M. Visaria, "Sex Ratios at Birth in Territories with a Relatively Complete Registration," Eugenics Quarterly, XIV, 1967, pp. 132-142; Ingrid Waldron, "The Role of Genetic and Biological Factors in Sex Differences in Mortality," in Alan Lopez and Lado Ruzicka, eds., Sex Differentials in Mortality: Trends, Determinants, and Consequences, Department of Demography, Miscellaneous Series, No. 4 (Canberra, Australia: Australian National University, 1983).

6. Sex ratios for large juvenile populations above 105.0 require explanation since 105.0 is roughly the upper limit of what could be expected under "natural" conditions, that is, without cultural interference. We use the term "normal" in this paper to refer to sex ratios within a

"naturally" expectable range.

7.   In this discussion, we ignore possible age misreporting and treat the census age data as essentially accurate.   Although there may be a tendency for people to round their ages to the nearest zero, we feel that this kind of error in the Sri Lankan census is quite minor and would have only a negligible influence on our analysis. For details, see Department of Census and Statistics (Sri L a n k a) , Census of Population, 1971, Sri Lanka: General Report (Colombo: Department of Census and Statistics, 1978), pp. 67-69 (this volume is hereafter cited as 1971 General Report). Also, see Dallas F.S. Fernando, "Changing Nuptiality Patterns in Sri Lanka," Population Studies, IXXX, 1975, pp. 179-190.

8.   T. Nadarajah, "The Transition from Higher Female to Higher Male Mortality in Sri Lanka," Population and Development Review, IX, June 1983, pp. 317-325.   See also Christopher M. Langford, "Sex Differentials in Mortality in Sri Lanka: Changes Since the 1920s," Journal of Biosocial Science, XVI, 1984, pp. 399-410.   Both sources document that overall, female mortality rates in Sri Lanka are lower than male mortality rates.   Differential mortality by gender, then, cannot account for the sex ratio variations in Sri Lanka at any age group.

9.   Pravin M. Visaria, The Sex Ratio of the Population of India, Census of India, Vol. I, Monograph X (Delhi: Office of the Registrar General, 1961); Narinder Oberoi Kelly, "Some Socio-Cultural Correlates of Indian Sex Ratios: Case Studies of Punjab and Kerala," unpublished doctoral dissertation, University of Pennsylvania, 1975; Miller, The Endangered Sex; Tim Dyson and Mick Moore, "On Kinship Structure, Female Autonomy, and Demographic Behavior in India," Population and Development Review, IX, March 1983, pp. 35-60; Stan D'Souza and Lincoln C. Chen, "Sex Differentials in Mortality in Rural Bangladesh," Population and Development Review, VI, June 1980, pp. 257-270.

10.   Ester Boserup, Woman's Role in Economic Development (New York: St. Martin's Press, 1970), pp. 85-86.   This extreme urban masculinization is reportedly found currently in only a few African countries (personal communication, Josef Gugler).

11.   Department of Census and Statistics (Sri Lanka), The Population of Sri Lanka (Colombo: Department of Census and Statistics, 1974), p. 41.   The census provides "singulate mean age at marriage" which is calculated from census data on proportions of the population by age who

were never married at the time of the census.

12. A.J. Selvadurai, "Kinship and Land Rights in the Context of Demographic Change," in James Brow, ed., Population, Land and Structural Change in Sri Lanka and Thailand (Leiden: E.J. Brill, 1976), pp. 97-112.

13. For an excellent case study of women in the coir (coconut fiber rope and matting) industry, see Carla Risseuw, The Wrong End of the Rope: Women Coir Workers in Sri Lanka (Leiden: University of Leiden Research and Documentation Center on Women and Development, 1980).

14. Miller has used a similar rate in an analysis of labor participation in rural India with the knowledge that, while such data do not accurately measure "work," they do provide insights into regional patterns of relative activity of males and females in the formal labor force. See Miller, The Endangered Sex, pp. 115-123.

15. Department of Census and Statistics (Sri Lanka), 1971 Census of Population, Vol. I, Part 3 (mimeographed; Colombo: Department of Census and Statistics, 1974), pp. 36-47. Additional details on estate-employed women are provided in: Diane Wolf, "Female Employment, Fertility and Survival Strategies in Sri Lanka," Staff Paper No. 80-16 (Ithaca, NY: Department of Agricultural Economics, Cornell University, 1980); and Christopher M. Langford, "The Fertility of Tamil Estate Workers in Sri Lanka," No. 31 (London: World Fertility Survey, 1982).

16. In contrast, Tamil regions in India exhibit high rates of female labor participation, see Miller, The Endangered Sex, chapter 5. Information on caste differentials in women's labor participation is provided in an excellent study of Tamil women in a village on the Jaffna peninsula: Else Skjønsberg, A Special Caste? Tamil Women of Sri Lanka (London: Zed Press, 1983).

17. A careful description of the limited nature of women's agricultural work in a settlement village of the Dry Zone is provided in Joke Schrijvers, Mothers for Life: Motherhood and Marginalization in the North Central Province of Sri Lanka (Delft, Netherlands: Eburon, 1985).

18. Raghnild Lund, "Women and Development Planning in Sri Lanka," Geografiska Annaler, LXIII, 1981, pp. 95-108.

19. See David E. Sopher, "Female Migration in Monsoon Asia: Notes from an Indian Perspective," Peasant Studies, X, Summer 1983, pp. 289-300.

20. This pattern is closely related to lower fertility in southwestern districts. See Langford, "Fertility Change in Sri Lanka."

3

Rising Suicide Rates

A dramatic rise in the incidence of suicide has occurred in Sri Lanka since the 1950s. Between 1950 and 1980, the number of suicides in the nation increased by 860 percent, while during the same period the aggregate rate of suicide climbed from 6.5 to 29.0 per 100,000 population. Marked increases in suicide rates were recorded for both sexes, most age groups, and all of the nation's administrative districts. Within three decades Sri Lanka's suicide rate jumped from moderately low to extremely high relative to suicide rates of other nations.[1]. The national suicide rate in Sri Lanka may be the highest in Asia. Even Japan, with its very high rate in 1979 of 18.0 was far behind Sri Lanka.[2] Thailand, in comparison, had a suicide rate of 4.9 in 1976.[3] In certain small island nations of the Pacific extremely high suicide rates were registered, nearing those of Sri Lanka. For instance, the average rate in Western Samoa between 1981 and 1983 was 22.6,[4] approximating the rate in Sri Lanka during the mid-1970s.

We have elsewhere examined the rise in suicide rates in Sri Lanka, focusing on the two decades 1955-1974.[5] In that paper we suggested a number of accompanying societal changes as possible explanations for the startling rise in the incidence of suicide. At least since Durkheim's famous study of suicide nearly a century ago,[6] sharp increases in suicide rates within a society have been viewed as indicators of societal stress and disruption. In this chapter, we probe more deeply into the regional variations, and gender and age distribution patterns in suicide rates over the years between 1950 and 1980. Our goal is to explore the possible association between the incidence of suicide and the magnitude and character of internal migration.

Other analysts have addressed the complex relationships between migration and mental health, and specifically migration and suicide. One interpretation which applies to certain social contexts is that out-migration can be an alternative to suicide. In situations of high population density and unemployment which frustrate aspirations and block social mobility, out-migration may be a solution for those who manage to move, while suicide may be a resort for those who cannot.[7] Others have examined rates and patterns of suicide among international migrants, viewing migration as in itself creating higher risk of suicide. A finding in some studies is that migrants have higher rates of suicide than the indigenous population, although other studies have found the opposite.[8] One study which considers the relationship between internal migration and mental health in the Philippines has documented higher levels of hypertension among migrants than among non-migrants.[9]

THE INCREASE IN SUICIDES

Throughout Asia suicide rates have been rising during the twentieth century, dramatically in some countries such as Japan, and only slightly in others such as Thailand. Various explanations have been proposed for this general upward trend, most of which revolve around accelerating modernization and attendant social change which conflicts with traditional lifestyles and values. Often cited also are the effects of declines in the economy which raise unemployment levels. These factors, as will be seen below, seem generally applicable to Sri Lanka. Our analysis of detailed data on suicides regionally, by sex, and by age group provide the basis for a more refined understanding of the sociocultural dynamics related to suicide in Sri Lanka.

The sharp increase in suicide rates in Sri Lanka is probably not explicable in terms of any single factor or identifiable cluster of factors, but is most likely linked to a profound disruption of the social environment due to the pyramiding of many facets of social change after the 1940s. Nonetheless, one of the components of social change over this period, internal migration, merits further study. We are able only to identify the districts in which suicides occur and, using census data, to point to certain demographic characteristics of those districts. Without information on the backgrounds and personal circumstances of the persons commiting suicidal acts or on discrete segments of district populations in which these acts occur, we are aware that we are playing a hazardous game with the "ecological fallacy." The variations in district suicide rates, however, are sufficiently compelling to tempt us to tread cautiously on the fringes of the "ecological fallacy," ever mindful that we are suggesting rather than specifying possible causal linkages.

Numbers of suicides by sex for the nation, for districts, and for age groups were obtained from the Statistical Branch of the Department of the Registrar-General in Colombo.[10] Rates, unless otherwise indicated, were calculated using the estimates of midyear population contained in the statistical abstracts issued annually by Sri Lanka's Department of Census and Statistics.[11]

The numbers and rates of suicides in the years from 1950 through 1980 for the nation appear in Table 3.1, and the changes in rates are depicted in Figure 3.1. The incidence of suicide for both males and females rose steadily and sharply throughout these years. In the mid 1970s, the rates for males dipped slightly from a peak at the beginning of the decade of about 30 per 100,000 population. At the end of the decade, however, the rates soared to new record heights. Female suicide rates continued steadily upward with few reversals or plateaux after the 1950s.

DISTRICT VARIATIONS

Suicide rates by district[12] for selected years appear in Table 3.2. Because certain districts experienced rapid population growth that is not reflected in the midyear district population estimates, the suicide rates for the years 1975-1980 were determined on the basis of population figures obtained by calculating the average annual district population growth between the censuses of 1971 and 1981 and adding to the 1971 population base the average increase for each year after 1971.[13] Since 1950, the rate of suicide has risen in every district, in most cases by substantial margins. In each year, however, the differential in rates between districts has been very large. The north-central Dry Zone districts of Vavuniya, Polonnaruwa, and Anuradhapura generally were among the districts registering the highest rates, and the southwestern Wet Zone districts of Colombo, Kalutara, Galle, Matara, and Kegalle

TABLE 3.1
Numbers and rates of suicides, 1950-1980

Year	Number			Rate (per 100,000 population)		
	Total	Males	Females	Total	Males	Females
1950	497	340	157	6.5	8.3	4.4
1951	572	389	183	7.3	9.3	5.0
1952	551	357	194	6.8	8.3	5.1
1953	574	410	164	6.9	9.4	4.2
1954	669	449	220	7.9	10.0	5.5
1955	604	420	184	6.9	9.1	4.5
1956	699	504	195	7.8	10.7	4.6
1957	737	540	197	8.0	10.4	4.5
1958	777	580	197	8.3	11.7	4.4
1959	792	549	243	8.2	10.8	5.3
1960	977	693	284	9.9	13.3	6.1
1961	985	682	303	9.7	12.7	6.3
1962	1,214	891	321	11.6	16.3	6.5
1963	1,294	956	338	12.2	17.4	6.6
1964	1,602	1,130	472	14.7	20.4	9.2
1965	1,526	1,086	440	13.7	18.7	8.2
1966	1,523	1,103	467	13.6	18.6	8.5
1967	1,980	1,417	563	17.3	23.3	10.0
1968	2,062	1,496	566	17.6	24.0	9.8
1969	2,421	1,745	676	19.8	27.4	11.5
1970	2,392	1,685	707	19.1	25.9	11.8
1971	2,318	1,655	650	18.4	25.5	10.6
1972	2,698	1,998	700	21.0	30.1	11.1
1973	2,879	2,029	850	22.0	30.1	13.4
1974	2,938	2,066	864	22.1	30.3	13.4
1975	2,636	1,765	871	19.5	25.4	13.3
1976	2,795	1,819	976	20.4	25.8	14.6
1977	2,788	1,793	995	20.0	25.0	14.7
1978	3,012	1,946	1,066	21.2	26.7	15.5
1979	3,632	2,421	1,211	25.1	32.5	17.2
1980	4,272	2,860	1,412	29.0	37.7	19.7

Source: Derived from data obtained from the Department of the Registrar-General.

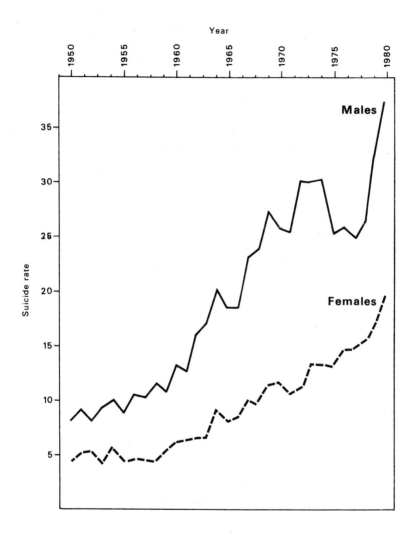

Figure 3.1   Suicide rates by sex, 1950-1980

TABLE 3.2
Suicide rates by district, selected years[a]

District[b]	1950	1955	1960	1965	1970	1975	1976	1977	1978	1979	1980
Vavuniya	34.6	17.9	21.3	18.9	59.8	61.5	57.7	52.9	49.2	40.1	84.1[c]
Polonnaruwa	d	d	31.6	32.8	24.6	31.5	35.2	47.1	45.1	53.1	50.2
Kurunegala	6.6	4.8	12.9	18.0	25.0	35.0	30.8	34.0	35.4	48.0	58.9
Anuradhapura	8.0	3.8	9.5	11.0	22.2	15.6	29.3	38.8	40.5	39.8	48.4
Jaffna	9.7	13.1	21.3	19.0	27.0	36.2	35.7	31.1	32.9	27.4	27.4
Hambantota	7.1	7.5	5.9	6.2	23.5	18.5	25.9	23.8	25.3	38.1	53.6
Mannar	2.8	4.3	5.6	12.5	24.3	26.4	36.4	29.8	37.1	25.9	25.1
Nuwara Eliya	3.4	7.0	5.3	14.9	18.4	20.0	28.2	27.4	23.1	36.7	44.3
Batticaloa	4.9	5.7	10.8	15.7	25.6	26.2	23.8	25.6	31.1	28.2	39.9
Matale	8.6	11.0	9.5	16.2	22.0	22.0	23.8	19.4	27.0	32.7	36.2
Badulla	4.0	6.7	15.1	22.2	24.9	22.5	23.0	17.2	22.4	34.4	37.8
Puttalam	7.3	7.3	6.4	19.9	25.0	24.3	28.7	17.4	22.2	22.5	30.7
Ratnapura	7.6	8.9	9.8	16.0	31.3	23.8	20.1	24.1	24.0	26.9	24.0
Monaragala	e	e	e	17.5	20.0	23.7	23.4	17.5	21.3	22.5	28.4
Trincomalee	5.3	8.7	21.1	6.0	12.0	17.6	23.4	22.7	23.7	25.5	21.6
Amparai	f	f	f	18.1	14.3	19.1	15.7	17.2	18.6	23.8	26.5
Kandy	6.0	5.1	7.1	12.8	19.7	19.8	9.7	18.0	18.2	23.7	25.8
Matara	4.8	2.7	8.3	9.0	7.5	15.7	18.2	16.4	17.4	19.1	23.0
Kegalle	5.5	4.9	10.7	16.0	21.1	14.6	16.2	17.4	14.2	17.2	23.0

TABLE 3.2 (continued)

District[b]	1950	1955	1960	1965	1970	1975	1976	1977	1978	1979	1980
Galle	6.1	7.8	8.9	11.6	17.3	12.5	15.1	11.8	15.0	19.0	18.6
Kalutara	8.9	9.8	10.5	12.0	17.5	12.5	10.9	12.9	10.5	11.6	11.7
Colombo	6.6	6.7	6.4	8.2	9.5	10.7	8.3	8.1	9.8	6.6	13.7[g]
Sri Lanka	6.6	6.9	9.9	13.7	19.1	19.4	20.3	19.9	21.2	25.2	29.2

Source: Derived from data obtained from the Department of the Registrar-General.

[a] For 1975-1980 rates were calculated using district population figures obtained by adding to the 1971 population for each year the average annual 1971-1981 population growth.

[b] Ordered highest to lowest 1975-1980 average suicide rate.

[c] Includes Mullaitivu district. The suicide rate for Mullaitivu was 89.3 and for the truncated Vavuniya district 80.1.

[d] Included in Anuradhapura district.

[e] Included in Badulla district.

[f] Included in Batticaloa district.

[g] Includes Gampaha district. The suicide rate for Gampaha was 9.8 and for the new Colombo district 16.9.

consistently were among those with the lowest rates of suicide in the nation. Furthermore, the differential between the higher and lower district suicide rates has widened over the years. Excluding Vavuniya, which frequently has recorded astonishingly high suicide rates, district suicide rates varied between 9.7 and 2.8 in 1950 and between 13.1 and 2.7 in 1955, but the range was from 53.1 to 6.6 in 1979 and from 58.9 to 11.7 in 1980.

In each of the years 1971-1980, Vavuniya and Polonnaruwa were among the five districts with the highest rates of suicide in the nation. In nine of those ten years, Vavuniya registered the highest rates of any of the 22 districts. Anuradhapura, Jaffna, and Mannar were also frequently among the districts with the highest suicide rates. Colombo, Kalutara, and Galle were in each of those years among the five districts with the lowest rates of suicide, joined by Matara in nine of the ten years and Kegalle in seven.

Vavuniya (including Mullaitivu in 1980),[14] Polon-naruwa, Kurunegala, Jaffna, Mannar, and Anuradhapura had the highest average district suicide rates for the decade 1971-1980, all above 30 per 100,000 population. Vavuniya, indeed, averaged a 61.4 suicide rate over the decade. All except Jaffna and Kurunegala are Dry Zone districts that experienced very rapid population growth during the period. Colombo (including Gampaha in 1980), Kalutara, Galle, Matara, and Kegalle districts clustered in the southwestern corner of the island exhibited the lowest average 1971-1980 suicide rates, under 18 per 100,000 population.

An imperfect but nonetheless apparent association between rapid population growth and a high incidence of suicide by district is suggested in Figure 3.2, in which average district suicide rates for the period 1971-1980 are plotted against 1971-1981 population growth rates. A drift from high growth and suicide rates in the upper right to low growth and suicide rates in the lower left of the figure is discernible. Major deviations from the pattern are caused by Kurunegala and Jaffna (Nos. 11 and 12 in Figure 3.2), both with population growth rates of under 2.0, the only districts that combined average suicide rates of above 30 per 100,000 population with population growth rates of less than 4.0 for the decade, and by Nuwara Eliya (No. 1), the only district to record negative population growth in 1971-1981. Of the six districts with population growth rates above 4.0, four had average suicide rates in excess of 30. The exceptions were Monaragala and Amparai

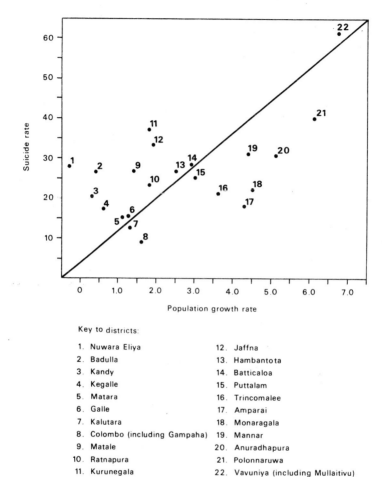

Key to districts:

1. Nuwara Eliya
2. Badulla
3. Kandy
4. Kegalle
5. Matara
6. Galle
7. Kalutara
8. Colombo (including Gampaha)
9. Matale
10. Ratnapura
11. Kurunegala

12. Jaffna
13. Hambantota
14. Batticaloa
15. Puttalam
16. Trincomalee
17. Amparai
18. Monaragala
19. Mannar
20. Anuradhapura
21. Polonnaruwa
22. Vavuniya (including Mullaitivu)

Figure 3.2 Average suicide rate, 1971-1980, and average annual population growth rate, 1971-1981, by district

(Nos. 17 and 18) with population growth rates of about 4.5 and average suicide rates bracketing 20. The two districts with the highest population growth rates, Vavuniya and Polonnaruwa (Nos. 21 and 22), also had the highest average suicide rates. Districts with suicide rates below 20 tended to cluster in the lower left of the figure, with population growth rates of less than 2.0 (Nos. 4-8).

SEX DIFFERENTIALS

In order to explore in more depth the variations in suicide rates between districts, it is advantageous to distinguish between male and female rates of suicide. District estimates of population do not distinguish between males and females, therefore we have calculated approximate suicide rates by gender for districts in selected years by disaggregating estimated district populations on the basis of the sex ratio of the district at the closest census (Table 3.3).[15]

The most striking feature of the suicide rates presented in Table 3.3 is the parallel pattern of male and female rates. Districts with high suicide rates for one sex generally have had high rates for the other sex and low rates for one sex have usually been accompanied by low rates for the other. Male and female 1980 suicide rates are highly and positively correlated (r = .85). In 1980, Vavuniya, Polonnaruwa, Anuradhapura, and Hambantota were among the five districts with the highest suicide rates for males and also among the five with the highest rates for females, while Galle, Colombo, and Kalutara were again among the five districts with the lowest rates for each sex.

The northern and north-central Dry Zone districts have registered very high suicide rates for both sexes and, although rates for males are in almost all cases higher than the rates for females, the difference in rates between the sexes has not been great. In the southwestern Wet Zone districts, in contrast, greater disparities exist between male and female suicide rates, with rates for males frequently twice the magnitude of the female rates. In other words, in those districts with the highest aggregate (both sexes combined) suicide rates, very high rates are found for both sexes; in districts with low aggregate rates, male rates of suicide are low relative to other districts but female rates are yet lower relative to the

TABLE 3.3
Approximate suicide rates by district and sex, selected years

District	1955 Males	1955 Females	1965 Males	1965 Females	1970 Males	1970 Females	1975[a] Males	1975[a] Females	1980[a] Males[b]	1980[a] Females[b]
Vavuniya	13.3	24.2	21.3	15.8	68.5	49.0	74.0	46.0	90.1	77.1
Polonnaruwa	[c]	[c]	36.9	27.2	26.6	22.2	33.7	28.7	58.1	40.0
Kurunegala	7.1	2.2	28.0	7.4	36.2	13.1	47.3	22.0	81.1	36.3
Anuradhapura	6.4	2.5	15.3	5.8	30.3	13.0	18.7	12.0	59.7	35.7
Jaffna	14.8	10.8	27.1	10.9	36.7	17.4	47.3	25.3	42.2	12.8
Hambantota	9.0	5.9	8.0	4.2	34.0	12.4	19.3	17.6	64.6	42.2
Mannar	3.6	5.2	20.2	3.5	30.1	17.6	21.3	32.2	30.8	18.6
Nuwara Eliya	8.4	5.5	21.0	8.1	24.1	12.5	24.2	15.7	53.7	34.8
Batticaloa	8.2	2.9	23.0	7.9	29.8	21.1	28.3	23.9	40.9	38.8
Matale	14.2	7.2	18.5	13.8	28.3	15.3	28.1	15.5	44.8	27.5
Badulla	9.4	3.8	31.1	12.1	30.9	18.6	28.1	16.6	50.7	24.6
Puttalam	11.3	2.6	28.8	10.4	33.5	17.2	36.6	11.2	46.8	14.3
Ratnapura	12.4	3.8	20.9	10.6	39.7	22.1	27.9	19.4	26.9	20.8
Monaragala	[d]	[d]	24.7	9.1	22.7	16.9	31.2	15.1	33.5	22.5
Trincomalee	11.0	5.3	7.1	4.6	18.4	4.8	16.2	19.3	26.1	16.4
Amparai	[e]	[e]	21.1	14.5	21.6	6.3	23.9	13.8	32.0	20.5
Kandy	6.6	3.5	18.2	7.2	28.2	10.9	27.9	11.4	35.7	16.1
Matara	4.0	1.3	14.0	4.0	11.4	3.9	22.3	9.4	31.1	15.5
Kegalle	6.4	3.3	21.5	10.2	30.7	11.0	19.7	9.3	37.6	8.7
Galle	11.6	4.2	13.9	9.4	23.3	11.5	17.9	7.2	26.1	11.5
Kalutara	11.2	8.4	15.3	8.6	26.7	8.1	18.6	6.3	15.3[f]	8.2[f]
Colombo	9.4	3.6	11.1	5.0	14.6	4.7	16.1	4.8	18.9	8.2

(continued)

TABLE 3.3 (continued)

Source: Derived from data obtained from the Department of the Registrar-General, 1971 General Report, and Census, 1981, No. 1.

[a] For 1975 and 1980 rates were calculated using district population figures obtained by adding the average annual district population growth in 1971-1981 to the 1971 population.

[b] Includes the new Mullaitivu district. Suicide rates for the newly delimited Vavuniya district were 89.6 for males and 69.4 for females and for Mullaitivu district, 90.8 for males and 87.3 for females.

[c] Included in Anuradhapura district.

[d] Included in Badulla district.

[e] Included in Batticaloa district.

[f] Includes the new Gampaha district. Suicide rates for Gampaha district were 15.0 for males and 4.6 for females; those for the truncated Colombo district were 21.9 for males and 11.3 for females.

male rates in the same district. In 1980, the highest district suicide rates for both sexes were recorded in Mullaitivu and the lowest in Gampaha. For males the Mullaitivu rate was 6.1 times that of Gampaha, while for females the Mullaitivu rate was 19.0 times that of Gampaha. The incidence of female suicide, hence, displays a more marked regional variation than that of males.

Female suicide rates by district display some association with age at marriage for women. Those districts in which female suicide rates are low relative to the national rates tend to be districts with higher average ages of marriage of females, and districts with high female suicide rates tend to correspond with the districts with lower female ages at marriage (see Chapter 2, Table 2.4). Districts with consistently very low female suicide rates (and low male rates as well) are southwestern Wet Zone districts, particularly the coastal districts, that are also characterized by the highest ages at marriage for females, moderately high female labor participation rates, male out-migration and female in-migration (see Chapter 2). However, female age at marriage is itself linked with a variety of social factors including ethnicity, level of education obtained, and employment opportunities for females and probably for males as well since unemployment is thought to be a major factor in delay of marriage. With available data, it is not possible to disentangle the effects on suicide rates of these various interlocking influences.

From our discussion in Chapter 1 of the dominant pattern of interdistrict migration in Sri Lanka it is evident that districts regularly registering the highest rates of suicide in the nation include the districts of the north-central Dry Zone that are characterized by rapid population growth rates, large proportions of in-migrants in their populations, and very high sex ratios. As discussed in Chapter 2, population growth rates by district are strongly correlated with the level of in-migration by district. In examining the possible correlation between the 1971-1981 rate of population growth by district and suicide rates in 1980, a moderate positive correlation ($r = .45$) was found for the suicide rate of both sexes combined, but a stronger correlation for females ($r = .51$) than for males ($r = .34$). Migration by district, as measured by the lifetime migrantion rate in 1971, is slightly more strongly correlated with 1980 suicide rates for both sexes combined ($r = .48$). Once again, the correlation is stronger with

the female suicide rate (r = .53) than with male suicide
rate (r = .38). Sex ratio tends to be more strongly
correlated with female suicide rates than male suicide
rates for both 1975 and 1980 suicide data.

AGE GROUPS

Suicide in Sri Lanka is predominantly a phenomenon of
youth. Since suicide data for the nation were first
recorded by age group in 1950, suicides have peaked in the
age range 15-29 years. Furthermore, the proportions of all
suicides accounted for by that age range have been rising
steadily. In every year after the late 1960s more than
half of all suicides have been committed by persons aged
15-29 years. Table 3.4 presents suicide rates for the
nation by age group and gender for selected years. The
rates of suicide have climbed over the years for both males
and females in all age groups except the oldest, and the
increase in rates is most marked in the years of the late
teens and twenties. Suicide rates peak by the mid-twenties
and thereafter decline, sharply for females and more
gradually for males until a second rise in the late years
of life. In the ages 15-19 years, female suicide rates
frequently surpass those of males, while in the ages 20-29
years, male suicide rates far exceed female suicide rates
(Figure 3.3).

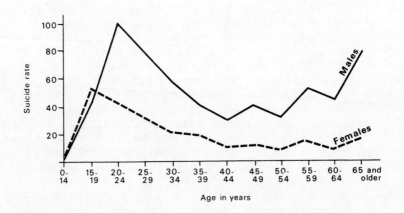

Figure 3.3 Suicide rates by sex and age group, Sri Lanka,
1980

TABLE 3.4
Suicide rates by sex and age group, selected years

Age (years)	1960 Males	1960 Females	1970 Males	1970 Females	1975 Males	1975 Females
0-14	0.2	0.4	0.8	0.7	2.0	1.1
15-19	11.8	14.1	30.6	35.7	25.5	33.5
20-24	26.7	18.5	71.5	32.3	56.1	39.9
25-29	22.3	7.3	56.2	18.5	45.9	19.8
30-34	15.4	7.9	29.6	12.1	29.4	15.2
35-39	16.2	9.4	35.8	12.0	36.4	13.1
40-44	15.9	2.9	31.3	12.7	23.9	6.2
45-49	20.2	6.0	31.7	12.0	30.2	7.4
50-54	13.9	5.2	27.4	8.3	35.5	8.4
55-59	33.1	8.7	49.5	8.1	39.2	10.2
60-64	37.4	9.0	36.4	7.3	38.8	10.4
65 and older	110.2	13.0	68.8	18.5	94.8	19.5

Age (years)	1978 Males	1978 Females	1979 Males	1979 Females	1980 Males	1980 Females
0-14	1.6	1.2	2.1	1.4	2.8	1.7
15-19	28.9	48.5	39.7	53.5	43.1	54.2
20-24	63.2	38.5	87.1	45.1	99.1	55.6
25-29	52.1	29.2	76.2	26.2	81.3	34.6
30-34	35.3	17.0	39.1	19.9	57.3	22.7
35-39	31.0	9.7	33.5	12.7	43.4	19.2
40-44	29.1	8.2	27.1	11.6	31.0	10.1
45-49	31.6	10.1	34.5	9.6	41.4	10.8
50-54	33.1	7.9	31.7	9.6	34.5	8.6
55-59	39.3	8.0	42.9	12.8	53.8	13.7
60-64	41.1	5.3	40.1	6.0	45.7	8.8
65 and older	70.8	16.1	70.3	16.5	79.4	16.8

Source: Derived from data provided by the Department of the Registrar-General.

SUICIDE IN SELECTED DISTRICTS

During the 1970s the Registrar-General's Department began recording data on cause of death (including suicide) by age group and gender within each district. While these data expand considerably the description of suicide that can be undertaken, they present a major challenge in effective presentation. Annual population estimates by gender and age groups for each district, from which suicide rates could be calculated, are not available.

We have selected for examination of suicide by age group and sex 10 districts representing the two extremes of the impact of internal migration. The two groups of five districts display markedly different characteristics relevant to migration (Table 3.5). The five districts with the largest percentages of 1981 residents born in other districts (lifetime in-migrants) also were the five

TABLE 3.5
Selected districts, with migration characteristics

District	Percent of 1981 Residents Born in Other Districts	Sex Ratio, 1981	Population Growth Rate, 1971-81	Lifetime Migration Rate, 1971
Polonnaruwa	48.3	129.8	5.1	42.54
Mullaitivu	42.7	122.8	6.3	---
Vavuniya	38.4	113.6	5.1	29.41
Monaragala	29.3	117.4	4.0	21.35
Anuradhapura	25.8	113.4	4.5	20.30
Kegalle	6.9	97.8	0.6	- 7.19
Matara	6.0	93.8	1.0	-20.34
Galle	5.7	93.9	1.1	-12.88
Batticaloa	4.9	102.4	2.7	- 3.07
Jaffna	3.2	98.1	1.9	- 8.90

Source: See Tables 1.1, 1.4, 1.6, and 1.10.

districts with the highest population growth rates in 1971-1981. Four, all except Mullaitivu which was not created as a separate district until the late 1970s, were among the five districts with the highest positive lifetime migration rates in 1971. All five districts were characterized by very high 1981 sex ratios. Since 1946, the areas currently contained in these districts have consistently registered growth rates well above the national average. The five districts with the smallest proportions of 1981 residents born in other districts all registered negative lifetime migration rates in 1971. Only Batticaloa was not among the districts with the lowest 1981 sex ratios. Kegalle, Matara, and Galle experienced a 1971-1981 rate of population growth below the national average. Among the districts with high proportions of in-migrants, Mullaitivu and Vavuniya, and of the districts with low proportions of in-migrants, Batticaloa and Jaffna have predominantly Sri Lanka Tamil populations. The other districts included in Table 3.5 all have predominantly Sinhalese populations.

For these five high and five low in-migration districts, approximate suicide rates by sex and age group for 1980 have been calculated by using the population figures from the census enumeration of March 17, 1981. The rates presented in Table 3.6, although not strictly comparable to rates based on district population estimates employed earlier, should be consistent within the table and comparable between districts. For the nation, the 1980 suicide rates calculated using the 1981 census figures are 37.9 for males, 19.3 for females, and 28.8 for both sexes. The respective rates obtained using the 1980 midyear estimates of population (Table 3.1) are 37.7, 19.7, and 29.0.[16]

A striking feature of the data presented in Table 3.6 is the similarity in the pattern of suicides over the range of ages for both sexes. None of the districts deviates markedly from the pattern of an early peak in the late teens and twenties, followed by a decline, swift for females and more gradual for males, until a second rise occurs among males in the oldest age groups. Only Galle district fails to display a major rise in the male rates in the advanced years. The high incidence of suicide in the years of late adolescence and early adulthood appears to be universal, characterizing districts undergoing rapid population growth as well as districts with stable populations, and including districts with predominantly Sinhalese populations as well as those with predominantly Sri Lanka Tamil populations.

TABLE 3.6
Approximate suicide rates by age group and sex, selected districts, 1980

Age (years)	Polonnaruwa		Mullaitivu		Vavuniya		Monaragala[a]		Anuradhapura	
	Males	Females	Males	Females	Males	Females	Males	Females	Males	Females
0-14	6.2	2.2	6.4	13.3	15.5	10.0	3.1	---	6.6	5.3
15-19	66.3	108.7	114.9	252.0	110.6	284.9	37.4	45.2	45.9	88.4
20-24	105.8	114.5	305.6	152.7	114.5	163.5	84.3	72.6	155.3	96.3
25-29	117.8	65.5	142.0	91.1	86.8	58.3	54.3	58.5	83.5	31.8
30-34	24.2	24.5	28.4	118.7	124.0	69.8	89.6	---	73.2	43.4
35-39	50.5	17.1	43.6	55.8	166.3	48.1	34.4	36.0	61.3	41.1
40-44	44.8	---	145.1	70.8	42.6	---	15.4	43.4	69.8	19.5
45-49	89.8	24.6	61.8	82.6	253.0	69.3	---	25.2	54.5	21.2
50-54	84.9	---	77.0	109.1	61.4	---	---	---	82.1	28.4
55-59	92.8	---	229.0	---	90.9	---	---	109.6	132.1	20.6
60-64	116.5	---	117.2	---	83.5	---	---	---	90.1	60.1
65 and older	102.1	79.1	169.3	256.1	313.3	---	42.7	---	136.0	17.1
All ages	56.0	38.3	88.3	81.4	84.2	66.9	29.7	24.4	57.2	34.8

TABLE 3.6 (continued)

Age (years)	Kegalle		Matara		Galle		Batticaloa		Jaffna	
	Males	Females	Males	Females	Males	Females	Males	Females	Males	Females
0-14	0.9	1.7	---	---	0.7	1.5	9.7	4.3	4.0	0.7
15-19	37.2	27.6	31.1	32.1	31.0	30.8	72.1	69.3	42.9	31.3
20-24	116.2	25.2	72.7	55.5	61.0	42.8	119.3	139.0	83.6	35.3
25-29	61.3	3.3	93.0	7.4	55.7	9.1	38.3	63.7	73.2	20.7
30-34	39.7	7.3	45.3	19.8	46.4	6.5	29.9	29.9	75.4	18.7
35-39	35.4	4.8	18.8	22.1	36.2	15.6	65.0	75.9	93.5	8.7
40-44	52.6	5.8	---	12.9	36.6	4.8	---	15.2	33.2	15.1
45-49	26.9	---	69.3	27.5	6.1	5.1	79.3	18.3	50.2	---
50-54	6.8	7.6	16.1	15.6	29.9	5.4	40.2	---	33.8	11.6
55-59	53.2	9.6	41.0	9.9	16.2	---	26.8	32.6	61.4	15.3
60-64	55.1	---	60.0	---	35.4	---	23.5	---	59.5	9.1
65 and older	107.7	13.6	61.6	10.6	37.1	16.1	117.7	44.6	79.6	---
All ages	37.3	8.7	30.8	15.4	25.5	11.6	4C.1	37.9	41.7	12.6

Source: Numbers of suicides are from the Department of the Registrar-General; population figures used in calculating rates are from Census, 1981, No. 2, Table 2.

[a]See Note 15.

Equally dramatic are the marked differences in suicide rates between the districts of high and low in-migration depicted in Table 3.6. The former districts are generally characterized by much higher suicide rates for both sexes in all age groups. Only Monaragala does not display the high suicide rates found in the other high in-migration districts. Particularly startling are the extraordinarily high rates of suicide for females aged 15-19 years in Mullaitivu and Vavuniya districts, exceeding the rates for all age groups of either sex in any of the ten districts except for 20-24-year-old males in Mullaitivu. It is noteworthy that in each of the five heavy in-migration districts female suicide rates exceed male rates, by very wide margins in all but Monaragala, in the age range of 15-19 years. In contrast, in four of the five low in-migration districts female suicide rates peak in the 20-24-year-age group, and for all five of these districts in the age range 15-19, female suicide rates are approximately equal to or lower than the rates for males.

MIGRATION, SOCIAL DISRUPTION, AND SUICIDE

The high rates of suicide for both sexes in rapidly growing Dry Zone districts raise the possibility of association between the disruptions of family and social bonds attendant on migration and suicide resulting, perhaps, from a sense of isolation and loneliness in the new area of residence. The high sex ratios of these districts indicate that many men migrate into the area without their families, as is also implied by the spouse separation rates presented in Chapter 2.

It seems likely that many migrants from the lush and green Wet Zone would experience difficulties in adjustment to the somber Dry Zone without family or village friends and kinsmen, perhaps compounded by disappointment of earlier expectations about life in the migrant settlement.[17] Male migrants unaccompanied by their families may be presumed to suffer loneliness and desolation as a result of separation from their wives and the absence of the solidarities and certainties of their natal villages. Women who accompany or join their husbands in the Dry Zone may experience a similar sense of isolation from the loss of support and assistance of village friends and relatives, both for companionship and for help with child care and other tasks. In addition, in settlement areas women's economic status and opportunities have been undermined by a tendency for males to receive titles to land and access to credit.[18] Women's traditional work in Dry Zone <u>chena</u> (slash and burn) cultivation has also been curtailed by the nature of the agriculture promoted in government-sponsored settlements.

Conditions in the Mahaweli scheme area were described in poignant detail by an anthropologist who conducted intensive fieldwork in both a traditional village and a settlement scheme village in the Dry Zone. A quotation from her study depicts the situation in the settlement village:

> Interviews with inhabitants of a hamlet [of recent migrants] in the H-area, in 1978, showed that women felt the quality of their lives to have deteriorated since they came to live in the colony a few years before....The women did not understand how the "<u>loku mahatturu</u>," the big gentlemen, had been induced to plan a colony like this. "We get crazy here," some said; "there is nobody here" (i.e., no relatives); "we do not live here as human beings but as wild animals." They could not cope with the problems of loneliness and poverty; and even less with the feelings of shame and loss of dignity. How had the "big gentlemen" planned all this, then?[19]

CONCLUSION

The general association in Sri Lanka of high rates of suicide for both sexes with the presence of large proportions of in-migrants and the accompanying skewed sex ratios suggests a causal linkage between migration and social disruption, leading to high and rising suicide rates.[20] Available data do not allow differentiation of the incidence of suicide between recent migrants and lifetime residents. However, it may be surmised that heavy migration results in disruption of the local community with possible unsettling consequences for the earlier residents as well as for the migrants.

Districts with low suicide rates have frequently been those characterized by considerable net out-migration, suggesting that migration and the prospect of a new start in another location may appear to be a solution to unemployment or other personal problems and, hence, an alternative to suicide. When the migrant encounters new sets of problems in the district of destination, however, the new frustrations and disappointments following on the old may create an intolerable level of stress or depression, heightening the prospect for suicidal acts. Admittedly, however, this line of argument can be offered as no more than a supposition at this time.

Dislocations and disappointments resulting from internal migration cannot explain the ubiquitous rise in suicide rates affecting all districts, both sexes, and most age groups. Furthermore, Monaragala and Amparai districts have experienced population growth through migration but have not displayed high rates of suicide. Over the past three decades Jaffna district frequently recorded high rates of suicide accompanied by considerable out-migration. Southwestern coastal districts characterized by male out-migration and female in-migration have regularly registered very low suicide rates relative to those of other districts and particularly low rates for females.

The universality of the rise in the incidence of suicide throughout Sri Lanka suggests forces of sweeping impact at work resulting in a general disruption of customary habits, practices, and relationships following on the rapid pace of social change. The situation in contemporary Sri Lanka recalls Durkheim's classic model in which mounting rates of suicide accompany or follow major dislocations of the social environment which lead to rising levels of anomie due to the confusion of the values and expectations that regulate social behavior and maintain the individual's integration within the social unit.[21] The disruptions of migration constitute an important contributing factor in the multiple social changes over the last three or four decades that have led to a fundamental dislocation of the more stable and predictable village society of the past.

NOTES

1. National suicide rates throughout the world range from less than 10 to more than 25 per 100,000 population: H.L.P. Resnick, "Suicide," in Harold I. Kaplan, Alfred M. Freedman, and Benjamin J. Sadock, eds., Comprehensive Textbook of Psychiatry (3rd ed.; Baltimore, MD: Williams and Wilkins, 1980), Vol. II, p. 2085. Suicide rates above 15 per 100,000 population have been classified as high and those below 5 as low by Robert J. Havighurst, "Suicide and Education," in Edwin S. Shneidman, ed., On the Nature of Suicide (San Francisco, CA: Jossey-Bass, 1969), p. 56.

2. Data on suicide in several Asian countries have been carefully compiled and presented in Lee Headley, ed., Suicide in Asia and the Near East (Berkeley: University of California Press, 1983).

3. Somporn Bussaratid and Sompop Ruangtrakool, "Thailand," in Headley, ed., Suicide in Asia, p. 147.

4. John R. Bowles, "Suicide and Attempted Suicide in Contemporary Western Samoa," in Francis X. Hezel, Donald H. Rubenstein and Geoffrey M. White, eds., Culture, Youth and Suicide in the Pacific: Papers from an East-West Center Conference, Working Paper Series, Pacific Islands Studies Program (Honolulu, HI: University of Hawaii at Manoa and the Institute of Culture and Communication, East-West Center, 1983), pp. 15-35.

5. See Robert N. Kearney and Barbara D. Miller, "The Spiral of Suicide and Social Change in Sri Lanka," Journal of Asian Studies, XLV (1985), pp. 81-102. For a more detailed examination of female suicide, see Barbara D. Miller and Robert N. Kearney, "Women's Suicide in Sri Lanka," in Patricia Whelehan, ed., The Anthropology of Women's Health (South Hadley, MA: Bergin and Garvey Publishers, forthcoming).

6. Emile Durkheim, Suicide: A Study in Sociology (Glencoe, IL: Free Press, 1951).

7. Cluny Macpherson and La'avasa Macpherson, "Suicide in Western Samoa: A Sociological Perspective," in Hezel et al., eds., Culture, Youth and Suicide in the Pacific, especially pp. 48-54.

8. Several interesting studies have been done on the topic of international migration and suicide patterns: A.W. Burke, "Socio-Cultural Determinants of Attempted Suicide among West Indians in Birmingham: Ethnic Origin and Immigrant Status," British Journal of Psychiatry, CIXXX, 1976, pp. 261-266; P.W. Burvill et al., "Attempted Suicide

and Immigration in Perth, Western Australia 1969-1978,"
Acta Psychiatrica Scandinavica, LXIIX, 1983, pp. 89-99; and
D. Lester, "Migration and Suicide," Medical Journal of
Australia, I, 1972, pp. 941-942.

9. Robert A. Hackenberg, et al., "Migration,
Modernization and Hypertension: Blood Pressure Levels in
Four Philippine Communities," Medical Anthropology, VII,
1983, pp. 44-71.

10. See Kearney and Miller, "The Spiral of Suicide,"
for further description of the data and discussion of
reliability. Also, see S.A.W. Dissanayake and W.P. de
Silva, "Suicide and Attempted Suicide in Sri Lanka," Ceylon
Journal of Medical Science, XXIII, June and December 1974,
pp. 10-17; and S.A.W. Dissanayake and Padmal de Silva, "Sri
Lanka," in Headley, ed., Suicide in Asia, pp. 167-209.

11. Department of Census and Statistics (Sri Lanka),
Statistical Abstract of Sri Lanka [title varies] (Colombo:
Department of Government Printing, annual), for the years
1960-1982. The midyear population estimates are calculated
by the Department of Census and Statistics by taking the
population at the preceding census and adding the natural
increase (excess of births over deaths) and adding or
subtracting the net gain or loss of population resulting
from international migration. Subsequent censuses have
confirmed the accuracy of the estimates for the nation as a
whole. However, in arriving at population estimates for
districts, the estimated national population is allocated
among the districts in the same proportion as at the last
census. Since some sparsely populated districts have been
experiencing rapid population growth as a result of
interdistrict migration, a distortion is introduced in the
district population estimates that increases in years more
distant from the last census. Consequently, we have for
certain purposes adopted an alternative method of arriving
at district population figures, as will be indicated.

12. The defunct districts of Negombo and Chilaw,
retained as separate reporting units in the Registrar-
General's figures, have been included with Colombo and
Puttalam districts, respectively, in all district data
discussed here. Also, to facilitate comparisons over time,
the new districts of Mullaitivu and Gampaha, for which data
were first separately available in 1980, have in certain
tables been included within Vavuniya and Colombo districts,
respectively, as is indicated in notes to those tables.

13. This method of arriving at district populations
is based the questionable assumption that growth occurred
at the same rate throughout the decade. Nonetheless, this

method appears to provide more nearly accurate figures for district populations in the fast-growing districts than the midyear estimates which assume that each district contains the same proportion of the nation's population as at the last census. For Polonnaruwa, for example, the 1980 midyear population estimate was 201,000, whereas the 1981 census enumerated a population of nearly 263,000 persons in the district. By the interpolation employed here, the 1980 population was calculated at slightly under 253,000 based on an average annual growth during 1971-1981 of 9,910 persons. For the nation as a whole, however, suicide rates calculated by the two methods produced virtually identical suicide rates (cf. Table 3.1 and Table 3.2).

14. The two 1980 districts of Mullaitivu and Vavuniya are not congruent with the earlier district of Vavuniya because of alterations of their boundaries with Mannar and Jaffna districts. Hence, the suicide rate for the combined districts for 1980 (the first year for which suicide data were available for each separately) is not exactly comparable with earlier rates for the undivided Vavuniya district.

15. Thus, sex ratios from the 1953 census were used to disaggregate district population estimates for 1955, those from the 1963 census for 1965, those from the 1971 census for 1970 and 1975, and those from the 1981 census for 1980.

16. The figures on population by district, sex, and age group from which the suicide rates were calculated are from Department of Census and Statistics, Census of Population and Housing, Sri Lanka, 1981: Population Tables Based on a Ten Percent Sample, Preliminary Release No. 2 (Colombo: Department of Census and Statistics, 1982), Table 2 (this publication is hereafter cited as Census, 1981, No. 2). Some discrepancies exist between district totals by sex in these figures, based on a 10 percent sample, and those from the full census enumeration (Census, 1981, No. 1, Table 1), with the latter figures considered by the Department of Census and Statistics to be the actual total figures for the districts (see Census, 1981, No. 2, p. iii). For all districts except Monaragala the discrepancies are slight and have little effect on the suicide rates calculated for the district population by sex. In the case of Monaragala, however, the figures based on the 10 percent sample show about 14,000 more males and fewer females from a total district population of almost 280,000 than do the presumed actual figures for the district. The resulting skew produces a lower apparent

male suicide rate for all ages (from 32.4 per 100,000 population calculated from the actual district figures to 29.7 calculated from the 10 percent sample figures) and higher apparent female suicide rates for all ages (from 21.8 using the actual population figures to 24.4 calculated from the sample figures). This skew may influence the suicide rates presented for any or all of the age groups in Monaragala district and should be kept in mind in evaluating the Monaragala data.

17. Psychological distress caused by loosening of the extended family bond has also been noted for India; see Sudhir Kakar, The Inner World: A Psychoanalytic Study of Childhood and Society in India (2nd ed., New York: Oxford University Press, 1981), pp. 120-121.

18. These problems for women in the settlement areas are clearly documented by Joke Schrijvers in Mothers for Life: Motherhood and Marginalization in the North Central Province of Sri Lanka (Delft, Netherlands: Eburon, 1985), especially Chapter 3; and Ragnhild Lund, "Women and Development Planning in Sri Lanka," Geografiska Annaler, LXIII, 1981, especially pp. 104-106.

19. Schrijvers, Mothers for Life, pp. 67-68.

20. Migration as a factor in undermining village social patterns and authority structures and promoting competition, conflict, and crime was noted by Gananath Obeyesekere, The Goddess Pattini and the Parable on Justice, Punitham Tiruchelvam Memorial Lecture, July 21, 1983 (Colombo: New Leela Press, 1983), pp. 18-19.

21. Durkheim, Suicide.

4

Ethnic Confrontation

There is little doubt that internal migration over recent decades has exacerbated ethnic tensions in Sri Lanka. The movement of population within the nation has been the subject of impassioned political contention for at least three decades, sharpened and dramatized by the growth over the past dozen years of a demand for a separate state on the island for the Sri Lanka Tamil minority. Our examination of consequences of internal migration turns in this chapter to the topic of ethnic conflict and confrontation. It is not possible to establish the precise degree to which migration may have contributed to the ethnic tensions and violence that have gripped the island. Rather, we present evidence of population movements which strongly suggests a role, in combination with other social and political circumstances and developments, in inspiring and fueling collisions between majority and minority ethnic communities.

THE ETHNIC COMMUNITIES OF SRI LANKA

Sinhalese constitute the majority of Sri Lanka's population, 74 percent in 1981. Nearly 13 percent of the 1981 population was composed of Sri Lanka Tamils, whose ancestors have populated the northern and eastern parts of the island since antiquity. Slightly less than 6 percent of the island's population consisted of Indian Tamils, so designated to distinguish them from the Sri Lanka Tamils. The Indian Tamils are descendants of migrants from South India who came to Sri Lanka in the nineteenth and early twentieth centuries and have resided principally in the tea-growing areas of the central highlands. In addition, a

community called Sri Lanka Moors, a name given the island's
Muslims during the period of Portuguese colonial rule,
constituted 7 percent of the 1981 population. Malays,
Burghers, and others collectively constituted less than 1
percent of the population.[1]

The association between ethnic community and religion
is very close. In 1946, 92 percent of all Sinhalese were
Buddhists, while 81 and 89 percent, respectively, of Sri
Lanka Tamils and Indian Tamils were Hindus. Virtually all
the remainder--8 percent of the Sinhalese, 16.5 percent of
the Sri Lanka Tamils, and 8 percent of the Indian Tamils--
were Christians. The Sri Lanka Moor community was 99
percent Muslim.[2] Subsequent censuses have not provided
comparable data, but it is unlikely that any major change
in the religious composition of the communities has
occurred, and such minor shifts as have occurred have
probably been in the direction of greater congruence
between religion and ethnic community. Based on the sizes
of ethnic communities and religious groups in 1971, the
Department of Census and Statistics inferred that about
93.5 percent of Sinhalese were Buddhists and 86 percent of
Sri Lanka and Indian Tamils were Hindus. Virtually all
Moors and Malays were presumed to be Muslims.[3]

The ethnic composition of district populations at time
of the census of 1981 appears in Table 4.1 (see Chapter 1,
Figure 1.1 for locations of districts). Sinhalese were a
majority of the population in all districts except the
seven districts of the Northern and Eastern Provinces--
Jaffna, Mannar, Vavuniya, Mullaitivu, Batticaloa, Amparai,
and Trincomalee--and Nuwara Eliya district in the central
highlands. Sri Lanka Tamils constituted a majority of the
populations of the four northern districts and Batticaloa,
and were substantial minorities in Amparai and Trincomalee
districts. Indian Tamils formed the largest single ethnic
group in Nuwara Eliya, constituting slightly less than half
the population, and were substantial minorities in several
other districts of the central highlands and in the North.
Sri Lanka Moors, although spread throughout the island and
a majority in no district, accounted for major proportions
of the population in the east-coast districts of
Batticaloa, Amparai, and Trincomalee and in Mannar in the
North.

TABLE 4.1

Ethnic   composition   of   Sri   Lanka   district   populations,   1981
(percent)

District	Sinhalese	Sri Lanka Tamils	Indian Tamils	Sri Lanka Moors	Others
Colombo	77.9	9.8	1.3	8.3	2.8
Gampaha	92.2	3.3	0.4	2.8	1.3
Kalutara	87.3	1.0	4.1	7.5	0.2
Kandy	75.0	4.9	9.3	9.9	0.8
Matale	79.9	6.9	6.7	7.2	0.3
Nuwara Eliya	35.9	13.5	47.3	2.8	0.5
Galle	94.4	0.7	1.4	3.2	0.3
Matara	94.6	0.6	2.2	2.6	0.1
Hambantota	97.4	0.4	0.1	1.1	1.1
Jaffna	0.6	95.3	2.4	1.7	0.1
Mannar	8.1	50.6	13.2	26.6	1.5
Vavuniya	16.6	56.9	19.4	6.9	0.3
Mullaitivu	5.1	76.0	13.9	4.9	0.2
Batticaloa	3.2	70.8	1.2	24.0	0.8
Amparai	37.6	20.1	0.4	41.5	0.3
Trincomalee	33.6	33.8	2.6	29.0	1.0
Kurunegala	93.1	1.1	0.5	5.1	0.2
Puttalam	82.6	6.7	0.6	9.7	0.4
Anuradhapura	91.3	1.2	0.1	7.1	0.2
Polonnaruwa	90.9	2.2	0.1	6.5	0.3
Badulla	68.5	5.7	21.1	4.2	0.5
Monaragala	92.9	1.8	3.3	1.9	0.1
Ratnapura	84.7	2.3	11.1	1.7	0.2
Kegalle	86.3	2.1	6.4	5.1	0.1
Sri Lanka	74.0	12.6	5.6	7.1	0.7

Source: Census, 1981, No. 1.

MIGRATION AND THE "TAMIL HOMELAND"

Basic to the Tamil demand for a separate state is the claim to a "traditional homeland" of the Tamils of Sri Lanka in the northern and eastern regions of the island, regions included in an independent Tamil kingdom in the thirteenth to seventeenth centuries.[4] The dominant pattern of migration within the island, as noted in Chapter 1, involves the movement of persons, mainly Sinhalese, from the densely populated southwestern Wet Zone to areas of the northern and eastern Dry Zone, including areas considered by Tamils to be within their traditional homeland. The progressive populating of the once sparsely settled Dry Zone has resulted in a blurring of the porous imaginary boundary that had long separated the predominantly Sinhalese and the predominantly Sri Lanka Tamil regions.

The migration of Sinhalese settlers into the northern and eastern Dry Zone, in part with government sponsorship and facilitation, has long been viewed by Sri Lanka Tamil leaders as constituting a threat to the continued existence of the ethnic community. At the founding in 1949 of the Federal Party, which in the 1950s was to become the principal political organization among the Sri Lanka Tamils, the party's leader denounced government sponsorship of colonization in the Dry Zone and warned: "If this policy is allowed to continue unchecked there will be no Tamil majority areas left in the course of a few decades."[5] A quarter of a century later, the Federal Party's successor organization, the Tamil United Liberation Front (TULF), issued a call for a separate Tamil state, to be named Eelam. Among the grievances cited to justify the call for separation was the contention that Sinhalese-dominated governments had made "serious inroads into the territories of the former Tamil kingdom by a system of planned and state-aided Sinhalese colonisation and large scale regularisation of recently encouraged Sinhalese encroachments [on public land] calculated to make the Tamils a minority in their own homeland."[6]

Tamil claims to the North and East have not gone undisputed. Typical of challenges from some sections of the Sinhalese was that of a Buddhist organization, which complained of Tamil assertions of the inviolability of the traditional Tamil homeland combined with Tamil freedom to reside in all parts of the nation:

Whilst the Northern Province is exclusively meant for the Tamils even according to the Thesavalamai Law [customary Jaffna Tamil law] obtaining there, the rest of the Island is the common property of all including Tamils. At present this claim is being extended to the Eastern Province as well, calling it a "Traditional Tamil Homeland" where no Sinhalese should settle down.[7]

Throughout the late 1970s and early 1980s, ethnic tension and conflict mounted, punctuated by communal riots in 1977, 1981, and 1983. At the same time, an underground guerrilla movement, called the Tiger Movement, sought the attainment of an independent Tamil state by violent means.[8] In late 1984 an incident occurred that starkly underlined the ethnic tensions associated with migration. The government reported the massacre, in two presumably related attacks, of at least 72 Sinhalese settlers in the northern district of Mullaitivu by "Northern terrorists."[9] Tamil sources claimed that the murdered Sinhalese settlers were former convicts and their families who had moved into the settlements after Indian Tamil refugees from the communal riots of 1983 had been forced off the Tamil-owned land by the army.[10] A few months after the massacre, the president of Sri Lanka, in an address to Parliament, charged:

the terrorists are attempting to shoot their way into the heart of Sri Lanka to the borders of what they call the State of EELAM. If we do not occupy the Border, the Border will come to us. We intend to act before they succeed.[11]

In an effort to seek resolution of a range of ethnic issues confronting the nation, an "All Party Conference" was convened by the president in early 1984 and met through the year. Among agenda items proposed for the deliberations was the statement:

A national policy on land settlement and the basis on which the Government will undertake land colonization will have to be worked out. All settlement schemes should be based on ethnic proportions so as not to alter the demographic balance [of the area] subject to agreement being reached on major projects.[12]

The talks were terminated at the end of the year
without accord, but further negotiations aimed at resolving
the communal conflict commenced in mid-1985.
Representatives of the TULF and five separatist guerrilla
organizations met with a Sri Lanka government delegation in
Thimpu, capital of Bhutan, in July. The Tamil spokesmen
sought acceptance of four principles, one of which was the
recognition of a territorially delimited Tamil homeland
within Sri Lanka.[13] Although the negotiations were
terminated the following month when four of the guerrilla
groups withdrew, the issue of a discrete Tamil homeland,
presumably insulated from penetration by large numbers of
non-Tamil migrants, remained in the forefront of the ethnic
confrontation.

In this chapter, we examine the ethnic composition and
changes in composition of Sri Lanka's northern and eastern
regions to determine the extent to which there have in fact
been significant shifts in the ethnic composition of the
regions' populations. As far as possible, we trace the
patterns of internal migration that have contributed to
such shifts. We also consider movements of Sri Lanka
Tamils within the island and trends in the degree of
concentration of the community in the traditionally Tamil
region. Finally, we examine the ethnic characteristics of
the area included in the proposed Tamil state of Eelam and
the implications in ethnic terms of the creation of an
independent or autonomous political entity in the North and
East. We thus seek to provide a detailed empirical
examination of one case of interaction between ethnic
pluralism and internal migration within a multi-ethnic
state, including some complexities which may arise from the
association of ethnic identity and ancestral territory with
a movement for political separation.

ETHNIC CHANGE IN THE NORTH AND EAST

The ethnic composition of the district populations in
the administratively defunct Northern and Eastern Provinces
at selected census years since 1911 appear in Table 4.2.[14]
In the 1960s, Amparai district was formed from the southern
and western portions of Batticaloa district and in the late
1970s, Mullaitivu was created from the northern part of
Vavuniya and a small portion of eastern Mannar. To
facilitate comparisons over time, Batticaloa and Amparai
districts have been combined, as have Vavuniya and
Mullaitivu districts.[15]

TABLE 4.2

Ethnic composition of northern and eastern district populations, 1911-1981 (percent)

	Sinhalese				Sri Lanka Tamils				Indian Tamils			
	1911	1946	1971	1981	1911	1946	1971	1981	1911	1946	1971	1981
Jaffna	0.1	1.1	0.9	0.6	98.3	96.3	94.9	95.3	0.3	1.0	2.6	2.4
Mannar	2.7	3.8	4.1	8.1	64.6	51.0	51.4	50.6	6.3	11.2	16.7	13.2
Vavuniya/Mullaitivu	10.7	16.6	16.8	11.4	77.7	69.3	61.3	65.4	3.4	4.2	14.5	16.9
Trincomalee	3.8	20.7	29.0	33.6	56.8	40.1	35.0	33.8	1.1	4.4	2.7	2.6
Batticaloa/Amparai	3.7	5.8	17.7	21.8	54.2	49.7	44.9	43.4	0.4	0.6	1.1	0.7
Total, North & East	1.8	4.9	11.0	13.2	81.6	75.5	67.1	65.1	0.7	1.7	3.5	3.6

	Sri Lanka Moors				Others			
	1911	1946	1971	1981	1911	1946	1971	1981
Jaffna	1.0	1.2	1.4	1.7	0.3	0.4	0.1	0.1
Mannar	33.2	30.1	25.3	26.6	1.7	3.9	2.5	1.5
Vavuniya/Mullaitivu	7.0	8.7	6.6	6.0	1.2	1.2	0.7	0.2
Trincomalee	32.0	29.2	31.9	29.0	6.2	5.6	1.3	1.0
Batticaloa/Amparai	39.2	42.0	35.4	33.5	2.5	1.8	0.8	0.5
Total, North & East	14.9	16.4	17.8	17.6	1.3	1.5	0.7	0.4

Source: See Note 14.

At the census of 1911, Sri Lanka Tamils were a majority of the population in the three districts then existing in the North and the two districts of the East. In the 70 years between 1911 and 1981, little change occurred in the ethnic composition of populous Jaffna district at the far north of the island, with Sri Lanka Tamils retaining an overwhelming majority. The other northern and eastern areas, however, have undergone some alteration of ethnic composition, most notable in the growth in the proportion of Sinhalese in Trincomalee and the Batticaloa/Amparai combination. The growth in the proportions of Sinhalese in Batticaloa/Amparai occurred after 1946 and presumably was related to government-sponsored settlements in the Gal Oya river basin, included in Amparai district since the 1960s. Equally dramatic is the growth in the Sinhalese proportion of the population of Trincomalee district, to one-third of the district's residents in 1981, equal to the proportion of Sri Lanka Tamils, who had in 1911 constituted a majority of the district population. Also evident from Table 4.2 is the steady growth in the Sinhalese proportion of the total population of the North and East, from less than 2 percent in 1911 and 5 percent in 1946 to slightly more than 13 percent in 1981. Conversely, the Sri Lanka Tamil proportion of the population of the North and East declined steadily, particularly after 1946.

Less striking or politically explosive is a slight growth in the proportion of Indian Tamils in the northern districts south of Jaffna. As employment opportunities on the tea estates of the central highlands stagnated, Indian Tamils filtered into the Tamil-speaking areas of the North, spurred by communal riots in 1977 that claimed as victims many Indian Tamils in the highlands. Riots in 1983 are thought to have given added impetus to this movement, as well as to Indian Tamil migration to South India, but these changes are not evident in the data now available. Sri Lanka Moors declined as a proportion of the population in the rapidly growing districts of the North and East, as members of other ethnic communities migrated into the districts.

A further look at the patterns of ethnic change in the districts of the North and East is provided in Table 4.3. The relatively small shifts in the ethnic composition of the region masked sizable changes in numbers as population growth after 1946 combined with heavy migration into the northern and eastern districts except Jaffna. In the 35 years between 1946 and 1981, Vavuniya/Mullaitivu grew in

TABLE 4.3

Population changes by ethnic community, northern and eastern districts, 1946-1981

	Population		Percent Increase 1946-71	Population 1981	Percent Increase	
	1946	1971			1971-81	1946-81
Sinhalese						
Jaffna	4,546	6,691	47.2	4,615	-31.0	1.5
Mannar	1,186	3,175	167.7	8,710	174.3	634.4
Vavuniya/						
Mullaitivu	3,870	15,981	312.9	19,824	24.0	412.2
Trincomalee	15,706	54,744	248.6	86,341	57.7	449.7
Batticaloa/						
Amparai	11,850	93,828	691.8	157,017	67.3	1,225.0
Total, North						
and East	37,158	174,419	369.4	276,507	58.5	644.1
Sri Lanka	4,620,507	9,131,241	97.6	10,985,666	20.3	137.8
Sri Lanka Tamils						
Jaffna	409,070	665,857	62.8	792,246	19.0	93.7
Mannar	16,076	39,977	148.7	54,106	35.3	236.6
Vavuniya/						
Mullaitivu	16,104	58,431	262.8	113,445	94.2	604.5
Trincomalee	30,433	65,905	116.6	86,743	31.6	185.0
Batticaloa/						
Amparai	101,061	237,794	135.3	312,663	31.5	209.4
Total, North						
and East	572,744	1,067,964	86.5	1,359,203	27.3	137.3
Sri Lanka	733,731	1,423,981	94.1	1,871,535	31.4	155.1

(continued)

TABLE 4.3 (continued)

	Population		Percent Increase	Population	Percent Increase	
	1946	1971	1946-71	1981	1971-81	1946-81
Indian Tamils						
Jaffna	4,194	18,033	33.0	20,001	10.9	376.9
Mannar	3,547	12,974	265.8	14,072	8.5	296.7
Vavuniya/						
Mullaitivu	967	13,828	1,330.0	29,358	112.3	2,936.0
Trincomalee	3,362	5,061	50.5	6,767	33.7	101.3
Batticaloa/						
Amparai	1,203	6,023	400.7	5,278	-12.4	338.7
Total, North and East	13,273	55,919	321.3	75,476	35.0	468.6
Sri Lanka	780,589	1,174,606	50.5	825,233	-29.7	5.7
Sri Lanka Moors						
Jaffna	5,159	9,785	89.7	13,757	40.6	166.7
Mannar	9,504	19,651	106.8	28,464	44.8	199.5
Vavuniya/						
Mullaitivu	2,028	6,327	212.0	10,417	64.6	413.7
Trincomalee	22,136	60,219	172.0	74,403	23.6	236.1
Batticaloa/						
Amparai	85,375	187,254	119.3	240,798	28.6	182.0
Total, North and East	124,202	283,236	128.0	367,839	29.9	196.2
Sri Lanka	373,559	828,304	121.7	1,056,972	27.6	182.9

TABLE 4.3 (continued)

	Population		Percent Increase 1946-71	Population 1981	Percent Increase	
	1946	1971			1971-81	1946-81
All Ethnic Communities						
Jaffna	424,788	701,603	65.2	831,112	18.5	95.7
Mannar	31,538	77,780	146.6	106,940	37.5	239.1
Vavuniya/						
Mullaitivu	23,246	95,243	309.7	173,416	82.1	646.0
Trincomalee	75,926	188,245	147.9	256,790	36.4	238.2
Batticaloa/						
Amparai	203,186	629,326	160.5	719,685	36.0	254.2
Total, North and East	758,684	1,592,197	109.9	2,087,943	31.1	175.2
Sri Lanka	6,657,339	12,689,897	90.6	14,850,001	17.0	123.1

Source: See Note 13.

population by nearly 650 percent, and Mannar and Batticaloa/Amparai registered growth of well over 200 percent. The largest percentage increases registered by Sinhalese between 1946 and 1981 were in Mannar and Batticaloa/Amparai. In Vavuniya/Mullaitivu, Indian Tamils increased in number from under 1,000 to nearly 30,000 between 1946 and 1981. Sri Lanka Tamils contributed the largest numbers to the population growth in Vavuniya/Mullaitivu. In the single decade 1971-1981, 55,000 Sri Lanka Tamils were added to the combined population of the two districts, compared to about 15,500 Indian Tamils and less than 4,000 Sinhalese. The slightly more than 113,000 Sri Lanka Tamils enumerated in the two newly demarcated districts in 1981 were nearly evenly divided between them, with almost 59,000 in Mullaitivu and less than 55,000 in Vavuniya. Sinhalese were more numerous in Vavuniya, where about 16,000 were enumerated, while about 4,000 were counted in Mullaitivu.[16]

Sri Lanka Moors did not figure greatly in the population dynamics of the North. The largest proportional increases of Moors in the North occurred in

Vavuniya/Mullaitivu, but Moors formed only 6 percent of the total population of the two districts. Sri Lanka Moors, however, continued to be a major element of the population in the east-coast districts.

In order to examine more closely trends in the East, data on Batticaloa and Amparai districts for censuses since 1963 are presented in Table 4.4. The ethnic composition of the population of Batticaloa underwent no significant change. In Amparai, however, Sinhalese increased steadily as a proportion of the district population, with both Sri Lanka Tamils and Moors registering declines in their proportions of the population. Between 1963 and 1981, 84,000 Sinhalese, 29,000 Sri Lanka Tamils, and 63,000 Sri Lanka Moors were added to the district population. In 1981, more than 146,000 Sinhalese were enumerated in Amparai, but under 11,000 in Batticaloa.[17]

The pattern of ethnic change that emerges from these data is one of growing numbers and proportions of Sinhalese in Mannar, Trincomalee, and Amparai. Sri Lanka Tamils, followed by Indian Tamils, led the population growth in Vavuniya/Mullaitivu. Between the censuses of 1946 and 1981, 97,000 Sri Lanka Tamils and 28,000 Indian Tamils were added to the population of this area. Jaffna and Batticaloa have remained ethnically unaltered and largely

TABLE 4.4
Ethnic composition of Batticaloa and Amparai district populations, 1963, 1971, and 1981 (percent)

	Batticaloa			Amparai		
	1963	1971	1981	1963	1971	1981
Sinhalese	3.4	4.5	3.2	29.3	30.2	37.6
Sri Lanka Tamils	71.3	69.1	70.8	23.2	22.2	20.1
Indian Tamils	0.9	1.7	1.2	0.6	0.6	0.4
Sri Lanka Moors	23.4	23.7	24.0	46.3	46.4	41.5
Others	1.0	1.0	0.8	0.6	0.6	0.4

Source: Department of Census and Statistics, Census of Population, Ceylon, 1963, Vol. I, Part 1 (Colombo: Government Press, 1967); 1971 Census, I, 1-22; and Census, 1981, No. 1.

Sri Lanka Tamil in population. In Jaffna district, Sri
Lanka Tamils accounted for 94 percent of the population
increase, which can be attributed to natural increase
rather than migration.

Figure 4.1 maps the Sri Lanka Tamil proportions of the
population in the northern and eastern districts at the
censuses of 1911, 1946, and 1981. Readily evident is the
shrinkage of the areas with large Tamil majorities. This
change should not, however, be construed as a crowding of
the community into Jaffna and Batticaloa. The absolute
numbers of Sri Lanka Tamils in each of the districts grew
considerably over these years, although the numbers of
members of other ethnic communities grew more rapidly in
several districts. The movement of Indian Tamils northward
can account for a part of the decline in the proportions of
Sri Lanka Tamils in the populations of the northern
districts other than Jaffna. However, the principal shifts
of population in ethnic terms are the result of growing
proportions of Sinhalese in the North and East, as depicted
in Figure 4.2. The penetration of Sinhalese into once
Tamil-majority areas is most evident in Trincomalee and
Amparai, although Sinhalese in 1981 represented a
significant minority in the truncated Vavuniya district.
While these maps suggest a territorial contraction of the
"Tamil homeland," Jaffna and Mullaitivu in the North and
Batticaloa in the East have remained overwhelmingly Tamil
in ethnic composition.

In 1985, an additional district, Kilinochchi, was
created in the North from the mainland part of Jaffna
district, leaving Jaffna district consisting only of the
peninsula, on which lived about 90 percent of the 1981
Jaffna district population. The administrative change has
no evident implications for the ethnic composition of the
region, but may symbolically suggest an isolation of the
peninsula, the heartland of the Sri Lanka Tamil community
which has produced most of the community's political
leadership. The new Kilinochchi district includes an area
in which nearly three-quarters of all Indian Tamils in
Jaffna district, about 15,000 persons, resided in 1981.
Sri Lanka Tamils, nonetheless, probably constituted 80
percent of the new district's population.[18]

Rapid district population growth largely as a result
of internal migration has not been limited to the once
predominantly Tamil areas. The population of the north-
central Dry Zone area currently contained within
Anuradhapura and Polonnaruwa districts jumped from 140,000
in 1946 to slightly more than 850,000 in 1981, including a

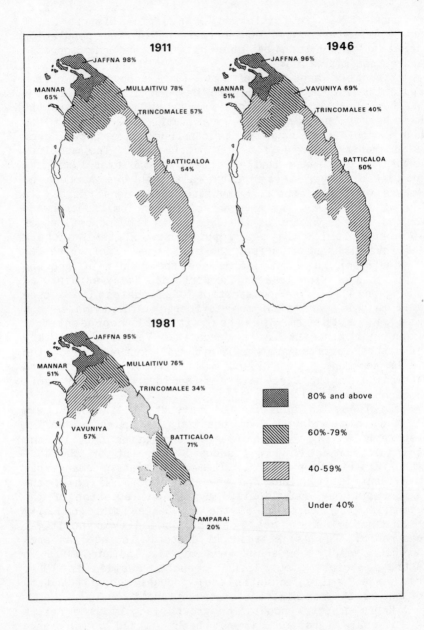

Figure 4.1   Districts of the northern and eastern
             provinces, showing Sri Lanka Tamil proportions
             of district populations, 1911, 1946, and 1981

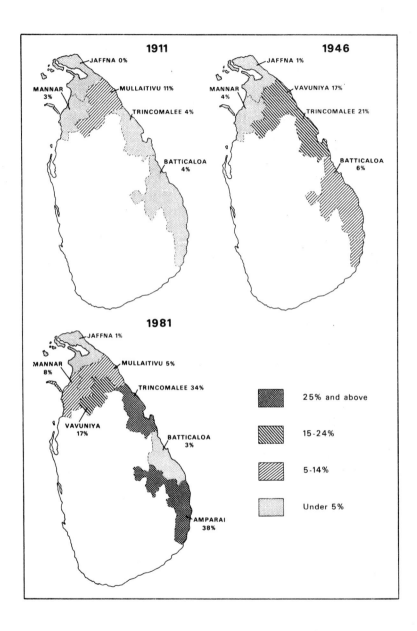

Figure 4.2 Districts of the northern and eastern
provinces, showing Sinhalese proportions
of district populations, 1911, 1946, and 1981

TABLE 4.5

Population born in districts other than that of 1981 enumeration, by region/district of birth (percent), northern and eastern districts

Region/District of Birth	District of 1981 Enumeration						
	Jaffna	Mannar	Vavuniya	Mullaitivu	Trincomalee	Batticaloa	Amparai
West and South[a]	33.1	40.9	23.6	19.6	41.7	27.2	52.5
Central[b]	38.7	15.3	31.4	22.3	28.8	25.0	35.6
North-Central[c]	6.2	2.8	6.6	3.4	5.1	3.5	1.6
Jaffna		31.5	30.7	47.2	12.9	16.7	1.0
Mannar	4.7		2.1	0.8	0.4	0.9	0.2
Vavuniya	3.0	2.7		2.5	0.4	0.6	0.1
Mullaitivu	2.3	0.3	1.8		0.1	0.3	---
Trincomalee	4.7	5.8	0.7	1.3		6.3	0.9
Batticaloa	5.4	6.6	1.2	0.8	7.1		6.4
Amparai	0.8	1.0	0.4	0.3	0.8	18.6	
Not Stated	1.2	0.8	1.4	1.8	2.8	0.9	1.7

Source: Derived from Census, 1981, No. 2, Table 19.

[a] Colombo, Gampaha, Kalutara, Galle, Matara, Hambantota, Puttalam, Kurunegala, Ratnapura, and Kegalle districts.

[b] Kandy, Matale, Nuwara Eliya, Badulla, and Monaragala districts.

[c] Anuradhapura and Polonnaruwa districts.

TABLE 4.6
Urbanization by ethnic community, northern and eastern districts, 1981 (percent of community)

	Jaffna	Mannar	Vavuniya	Mullaitivu	Trincomalee	Batticaloa	Amparai
Sinhalese	57.1	5.7	9.6	5.0	20.0	25.1	10.6
Sri Lanka Tamils	31.6	18.6	22.1	10.4	35.5	16.8	11.6
Indian Tamils	26.4	3.0	18.3	0.9	33.3	19.4	34.3
Sri Lanka Moors	88.5	11.8	22.6	18.1	42.9	43.8	17.3
All Communities	32.6	13.5	19.3	9.3	32.4	24.0	13.8

Source: Derived from Census, 1981, No. 1.

growth of nearly 300,000 in the decade 1971-1981. The influx was largely Sinhalese. Between 1946 and 1981, 665,000 Sinhalese were added to the area's population, pushing up the Sinhalese proportion of the population from 80 to 91 percent.[19]

Lifetime Migrants

Some inferences regarding ethnic patterns of migration may be obtained by examination of data relating to the district of birth of the 1981 population. In Vavuniya and Mullaitivu, about two residents in five were born in other districts, a proportion exceeded only by Polonnaruwa district (see Chapter 1, Table 1.1). Of seven districts in which more than 20 percent of the usual residents were born in other districts, four were situated in the North and East. The demographic stability of Jaffna and Batticaloa again emerges in the small proportions of residents of those districts born elsewhere, about 3 and 5 percent, respectively, the smallest proportions of all 24 districts. The northern and eastern districts (other than Amparai), hence, were located at the two extremes of the scale of lifetime in-migrants as a proportion of district residents.

In Table 4.5, the percentages of the population born in other districts by the district or region of birth are indicated for the northern and eastern districts. (In these data, the population base consists of all persons enumerated in the district, without regard to place of usual residence.) The population enumerated in Jaffna but born in other districts was very small. Jaffna in 1981, with a total population nearly nine times that of Vavuniya and 11 times that of Mullaitivu, contained fewer persons born outside the district than either Vavuniya or Mullaitivu. Jaffna has contributed significantly to the population of each of the other northern and eastern districts except Amparai. Although Table 4.5 gives no direct information on the ethnic community of migrants, the major contribution of the preponderantly Sinhalese districts of the West and South to the populations of Mannar, Trincomalee, and Amparai may be inferred to underlie the already noted change in ethnic composition of those districts' populations.

Urbanization

In the North and East, the populations of all ethnic communities have been largely rural as is indicated in Table 4.6 in which the urban proportions of each ethnic group are presented. The small numbers of Sinhalese and Moors resident in Jaffna district may be presumed to be engaged in business or governmental activities and, hence, display a relatively high rate of urbanization. Sri Lanka Tamils accounted for 92 percent of the district's urban population. The districts of rapid population growth-- notably Mannar, Vavuniya, Mullaitivu, and Amparai--have remained overwhelmingly rural and no ethnic group has been characterized by a high degree of urbanization. The Indian Tamils in Amparai accounted for only 1 percent of the small urban population of that district. From these data, it may be inferred that the population growth arising from in-migration has been largely rural migration for all ethnic groups.

SRI LANKA TAMIL POPULATION MOVEMENT

Changes in the ethnic composition of the nation over recent decades have not been great, as indicated in Table 4.7. The most marked change is the decline in the proportion of Indian Tamils in the population since the 1960s, and a consequent slight increase in the proportions of Sinhalese and Sri Lanka Tamils. Indian Tamils have been migrating to India under agreements between the Sri Lankan and Indian governments, and it is probable that some persons earlier classified as Indian Tamils reported themselves to be Sri Lanka Tamils after receiving Sri Lankan citizenship in the 1960s and 1970s. Between 1971 and 1981, the number of Indian Tamils enumerated fell from 1,175,000 to 825,000.

Sri Lanka Tamils have remained a relatively stable proportion of the island's total population but, as has been noted, have declined as a proportion of the population of several northern and eastern districts. This fact leads to the question of where the Sri Lanka Tamil population is located. In Table 4.8, the distribution of the community's population among the island's nine provinces is presented for 1911, 1946, 1971, and 1981. Provinces have been employed as the territorial unit in this presentation

TABLE 4.7
Ethnic composition of the population of Sri Lanka, selected
census years, 1911-1981 (percent)

	Sinhalese	Sri Lanka Tamils	Indian Tamils	Sri Lanka Moors	Others
1911	66.1	12.8	12.9	5.7	2.4
1946	69.4	11.0	11.7	5.6	2.2
1963	71.0	11.1	10.6	6.2	1.1
1971	72.0	11.2	9.3	6.5	1.0
1981	74.0	12.6	7.1	5.6	0.7

Source: Derived from Denham, Ceylon at the Census of 1911,
pp. 195-196; Census, 1946, Vol. I, Part 2, p. 105; Census,
1963, Vol. I, Part I, p. 23; Census, 1971, Vol. II, Part 1,
p. 25; and Census, 1981, No. 1.

TABLE 4.8

Percentage distribution of Sri Lanka Tamil population
by province, 1911, 1946, 1971, and 1981

Province	1911	1946	1971	1981
Northern	66.2	60.1	53.7	51.3
Eastern	19.0	17.9	21.3	21.3
Western	5.6	8.5	12.4	11.8
Central	3.5	5.5	5.6	7.9
Southern	0.3	0.9	0.5	0.6
North-Western	2.6	2.7	2.5	2.5
North-Central	1.1	1.3	0.9	0.7
Uva	0.7	2.1	1.6	2.2
Sabaragamuwa	0.8	1.0	1.5	1.7

Source: Derived from Denham, Ceylon at the Census of
1911, pp. 196-197; Department of Census and
Statistics, Census of Ceylon, 1946, Vol. I, Part 2,
pp. 105-106; Department of Census and Statistics,
1971 Census of Population, Vol. I, Parts 1-22, Table
9; and Census, 1981, No. 1, p. 3.

because of changes in the number and boundaries of
districts over the years (provincial boundaries in 1981 are
indicated in Figure 4.3).[20]

About 85 percent of the Sri Lanka Tamil population
lived in the Northern and Eastern Provinces in 1911,
whereas by 1981 the proportion of the community living in
those two provinces had declined to about 73 percent.
Jaffna district alone contained 61 percent of the island's
Sri Lanka Tamils in 1911 and 56 percent in 1946, but only
42 percent in 1981.[21]   In 1971, about one-eighth of the
Sri Lanka Tamil community lived in the Western Province
containing the city of Colombo. A slight dip in the
proportion found in the Western Province appeared in 1981,
possibly a consequence of communal riots in 1977 which may
have prompted some Tamils in the southwest to leave the
region for the North or East or to go abroad. The riots
were not, however, confined to the Western Province and
declines did not occur in other provinces of the Southwest.

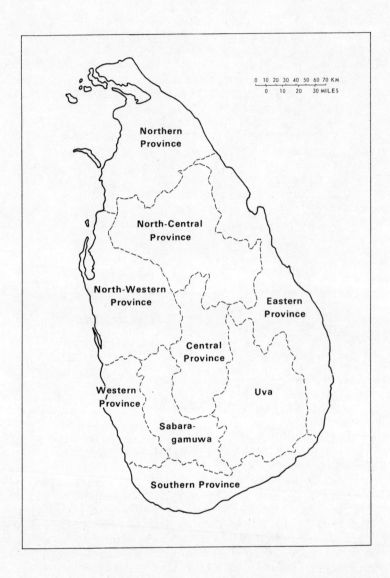

Figure 4.3 Sri Lanka, showing provincial boundaries

Nonetheless, in 1981 only Jaffna and Batticaloa districts contained more Sri Lanka Tamils than Colombo district. The increase in the proportion of Sri Lanka Tamils in the Central Province between 1971 and 1981 may be accounted for by a tendency for some persons formerly classified as Indian Tamils to designate themselves as Sri Lanka Tamils at the latter Census.[22]

It may be concluded that the Sri Lanka Tamil population has remained concentrated in the North and East, despite a decline in the proportion of the community living in the North over the years. While some growth appears in the proportion of Sri Lanka Tamils enumerated in the Central Province, the populous and urbanized Western Province has been the chief recipient of Tamil migrants from the North. In 1981, despite the communal violence of that year, nearly one-tenth of all Sri Lanka Tamils lived in the Western Province's Colombo district.

ETHNICITY AND THE PROPOSED EELAM

Sri Lanka is not unique in the modern world in spawning a demand for political separation made in the name of an ethnic minority claiming a territorial base within the existing nation-state.[23] Nor is Sri Lanka unique in that the ethnic geography of the island does not lend itself to simple demarcation of territories by ethnic group. Although alternate definitions of the boundaries of a proposed state of Eelam have appeared, the most common assumption appears to be that the prospective Eelam would include the four 1981 districts of the Northern Province and Trincomalee and Batticaloa districts from the Eastern Province, a territory of nearly 13,800 square kilometers (5,315 square miles), 21 percent of Sri Lanka's land area.

At the 1981 census, these six districts contained a total population of almost 1,700,000 persons, of whom three-fourths were Sri Lanka Tamils and one-eighth Sri Lanka Moors (see Table 4.9). Sinhalese constituted nearly 8 percent and Indian Tamils slightly more than 4 percent of the area's 1981 population. By religion, the population of the area in 1981 was 69 percent Hindu, 12 percent Muslim, 12 percent Christian, and 7 percent Buddhist. More than nine-tenths of the Christians were Roman Catholics, presumably mostly Tamils and found in greatest numbers in Jaffna and Mannar.[24]

TABLE 4.9
Population of the region associated with the proposed Eelam
(Jaffna, Mannar, Vavuniya, Mullaitivu, Trincomalee, and
Batticaloa districts), by ethnic community, 1981

Ethnic Community	Number	Percent of Region's Population	Percent of Ethnic Community in Region
Sri Lanka Tamils	1,280,888	75.4	68.4
Sri Lanka Moors	206,358	12.1	19.5
Sinhalese	130,136	7.7	1.2
Indian Tamils	74,066	4.4	9.0
Others	7,709	0.5	7.0
All Communities	1,699,157	100.0	11.4

Source: Census, 1981, No. 1.

Critics of an independent Eelam frequently have
charged that the creation of Eelam encompassing the
Northern Province and Trincomalee and Batticaloa districts
would produce a new set of minority problems.[25] Only
slightly more than two-thirds of the island's Sri Lanka
Tamils would be included in an Eelam so delimited unless a
major exchange of populations occurred. More than 590,000
Sri Lanka Tamils lived outside of this territory in 1981.
Moreover, the Eelam territory so defined in 1981 included
within it 206,000 Sri Lanka Moors, nearly one-fifth of all
members of that community. The sizable Sri Lanka Moor
population has its own traditional claim to residence in
the East. The problem posed for an independent Eelam by
the Moor minority in the area was dramatized by a 1985
outbreak of violence between Tamils and Moors that claimed
scores of lives in the Eastern Province.

If Amparai were added to the territory of the
projected Eelam, the area included would increase to 18,300
square kilometers (nearly 7,000 square miles), about 28
percent of the island's land area. On the basis of the
1981 census, the proportion of all Sri Lanka Tamils
included within its borders would rise to 73 percent.
However, this territory would also include 35 percent of

the Sri Lanka Moor community, and the Sri Lanka Tamil proportion of the territory's total population would drop to 65 percent while the Sri Lanka Moor proportion would climb to 18 percent and that of the Sinhalese to 13 percent.

The census figures do not reveal a deepseated division within the Sri Lanka Tamil community between the East-Coast Tamils and the Tamils of the North, particularly those of the Jaffna Peninsula. Distinctive patterns of traditional laws and customs, of social and economic practices, and of economic development and social change serve to differentiate the populace of the two regions.[26] The "Jaffna man" and the "Batticaloa man" are clearly recognized contrasting symbols among Sri Lanka Tamils (as is the "Colombo Tamil"). Differences of social and economic practice have also existed between the Tamils of the peninsula and those of the adjacent Northern Province mainland, although recent migration from the peninsula to the mainland has undoubtedly blurred the distinction. The Sinhalese-Tamil political confrontation and communal violence, however, may have overshadowed regional as well as religious and caste divisions within Sri Lanka Tamil society, at least in regard to the current demands for Tamil political ascendency in the community's traditional homeland.[27]

CONCLUSION

Considerable changes in the ethnic composition of the populations in parts of the North and East unquestionably have been occurring over the course of this century, most notably during the last three or four decades. The direction of change is toward larger proportions of Sinhalese among the residents of the sparsely populated and rapidly growing districts, accompanied by a decline in the proportions of Sri Lanka Tamils. The areas of large Sri Lanka Tamil majorities have been contracting over the years, leaving by 1981 only Jaffna and Mullaitivu (and presumably the new district of Kilinochchi) in the far North and Batticaloa in the East as districts of large Tamil numerical predominance. Sri Lanka Tamils in 1911 formed a majority of the populations of all districts in the Northern and Eastern Provinces. Since this is no longer the case, the territories of the "Tamil homeland" may be thought of as shrinking. However, it can be argued that in the far North and Batticaloa a "Tamil homeland" has remained intact, albeit of lesser territorial extent than the predominantly Tamil areas of the past. The ethnic shifts have not represented a constriction of the Sri Lanka Tamil community into an ever smaller territory. Considerable numbers of Tamils have moved from the Jaffna Peninsula to the nearby districts and to distant Colombo. The Sri Lanka Tamil community has (or had through 1981) progressively become more dispersed, with a declining proportion of the community residing in the North and East. Whether recent communal violence has reversed this trend cannot be determined from currently available data.

Although no direct information on the ethnicity of interdistrict migrants exists, it is evident from the data on district population growth by ethnic community that the immediate cause of ethnic transition in the northern and eastern Dry Zone is migration. The principal stream of migration is from the Southwest and involves the movement of Sinhalese into areas some, but not all, of which were formerly Sri Lanka Tamil in ethnic composition. A much smaller migration stream has brought Indian Tamils from the central highlands to the sparsely populated districts of the North. In addition, large numbers of Sri Lanka Tamils have moved from Jaffna to the other districts of the North and East and to the Southwest.

No attempt is made here to enter the political argument between Sinhalese and Tamil political leaders over the extent and inviolability of the "traditional homeland" of the Tamils of Sri Lanka. Whatever its political implications, there can be no doubt that considerable changes have been wrought in the ethnic map of Sri Lanka as a result of internal migration. The formerly nearly uninhabited areas of the Dry Zone had once served as a broad belt of demarcation between the Sinhalese and the Sri Lanka Tamils. Tamils have moved southward and Sinhalese northeasterly to populate the Dry Zone, seriously compromising the territorial demarcation of the ethnic groups.

Political contention between the Sinhalese and the Sri Lanka Tamils has involved many questions other than those of a territorial nature. Ethnic changes in regional populations have, however, fueled one major dimension of the ethnic conflict on the island, a dimension that may be of even greater moment if the drive for a separate Tamil state continues.

NOTES

1. Department of Census and Statistics (Sri Lanka), Census of Population and Housing, Sri Lanka, 1981, Preliminary Release No. 1 (Colombo: Department of Census and Statistics, 1981), hereafter cited as Census, 1981, No. 1.
2. Department of Census and Statistics (Sri Lanka), Census of Ceylon, 1946, Vol. IV (Colombo: Government Press, 1952), p. 275.
3. Department of Census and Statistics (Sri Lanka), Census of Population, Sri Lanka, 1971: General Report (Colombo: Department of Census and Statistics, 1978), p. 89. This volume is hereafter cited as 1971 General Report.
4. The importance of a sense of possession of a distinct territory, often including historical memories of its political independence, in the maintenance of the solidarity and self-identity of an ethnic group has been noted by George DeVos, "Ethnic Pluralism: Conflict and Accommodation," in George DeVos and Lola Romanucci-Ross, eds., Ethnic Identity: Cultural Continuities and Change (Palo Alto, CA: Mayfield Publishing Company, 1975), p. 11.
5. Presidential Address of Mr. S.J.V. Chelvanayagam, K.C., Delivered at the Inaugural and First Business Meeting of the Ilankai Tamil Arasu Kadchi (The Federal Freedom Party of the Tamil-speaking People of Ceylon) on 18th December, 1949, at the G.C.S.U. Hall, Colombo (Colombo: Ilankai Tamil Arasu Kadchi, n.d.), pp. 10-11.
6. "Political Resolution Unanimously Adopted at the 1st National Convention of the Tamil Liberation Front Held at Pannakam (Vaddukoddai Constituency) on 14.5.1976, Presided over by Mr. S.J.V. Chelvanayakam, Q.C., M.P." (mimeographed), p. 1.
7. Terrorism in North Sri Lanka and Racial Riots: An Analysis of Their Causes (Colombo: World Fellowship of Buddhists Sri Lanka Regional Centre, n.d. [1983]), p. 14.
8. On the Tamil separatist movement and the growing communal confrontation see Robert N. Kearney, "Ethnic Conflict and the Tamil Separatist Movement in Sri Lanka," Asian Survey, XXV, September 1985, pp. 898-917. On the social and ideological roots of the communal tensions see S.J. Tambiah, Sri Lanka: Ethnic Fratricide and the Dismantling of Democracy (Chicago: University of Chicago Press, 1986). For a militant separatist perspective see Satchi Ponnambalam, Sri Lanka: National Conflict and the Tamil Liberation Struggle (London: Zed Books, 1983). On

recent communal violence see Tamil Refugees Rehabilitation Organisation, Communal Disturbances in Sri Lanka (mimeographed; no place or publisher, 1980); Government of Sri Lanka, Report of the Presidential Commission of Inquiry into the Incidents Which Took Place Between 13th August and 15th September, 1977, Sessional Paper VII--1980 (Colombo: Department of Government Printing, 1980); and the essays contained in Part II of James Manor, ed., Sri Lanka in Change and Crisis (New York: St. Martin's Press, 1984).

   9.   Government of Sri Lanka, Northern Terrorists Massacre Innocent Farmer Civilians in Sri Lanka (leaflet; no facts of publication).

   10.   Reported in interviews by Kearney conducted in Colombo during March 1985.

   11.   Parliament (Sri Lanka), Parliamentary Debates (Hansard), Official Report, Vol. 34, No. 1 (Feb. 20, 1985), col. 15.

   12.   All Party Conference (Sri Lanka), "Annexure C," Statement of His Excellency the President and Chairman of the All Party Conference (Colombo: All Party Conference Secretariat, Dec. 14, 1984).

   13.   See Ministry of State (Sri Lanka), The Thimpu Talks: The Stand Taken by the Sri Lanka Government (Colombo: Department of Information, 1985), pp. 5-8.

   14.   Data presented in Tables 4.2 and 4.3 were derived from the following sources: E.B. Denham, Ceylon at the Census of 1911 (Colombo: Government Printer, 1912); Department of Census and Statistics (Sri Lanka), Census of Ceylon, 1946, Vol. I, Part 2 (Colombo: Government press, 1951), hereafter cited as Census, 1946; Department of Census and Statistics (Sri Lanka), 1971 Census of Population, Vol. I, Parts 1-22 (mimeographed; Colombo: Department of Census and Statistics, 1974), hereafter cited as 1971 Census, I, 1-22; and Census, 1981, No. 1.

   15.   The 1981 combination of Vavuniya and Mullaitivu is not precisely congruent with the earlier district of Vavuniya as some adjustments were made in the boundaries with Mannar and Jaffna districts.   The former district of Vavuniya was called Mullaitivu until the 1930s, when the district headquarters was moved to Vavuniya town and the district renamed.   In 1978, a separate Mullaitivu district was created.

   16.   Census, 1981, No. 1.

   17.   Department of Census and Statistics (Sri Lanka), Census of Population, Ceylon, 1963, Vol. I, Part 1 (Colombo: Government Press, 1967), hereafter cited as 1963 Census; 1971 Census, I, 1-22; and Census, 1981, No. 1.

18. The mainland Karachchi assistant government agent's division, which became a part of the new Kilinochchi district, in 1981 contained slightly more than 12,000 Indian Tamils, with Poonakari assistant government agent's division and the Kilinochchi town council area, also included in the new district, adding about 2,500 more. Jaffna district in 1981 contained an Indian Tamil population of 20,000. The areas grouped in the new district held a 1981 total population of about 82,000, including about 65,000 Sri Lanka Tamils (calculated from Census, 1981, No. 1, pp. 14-15).

19. Census, 1946; 1971 Census, I, 1-22; Census, 1981, No. 1.

20. The 1981 districts included in the provinces were: Northern Province--Jaffna, Mannar, Vavuniya, and Mullaitivu; Eastern Province--Trincomalee, Batticaloa, and Amparai; Western Province- Colombo, Kalutara, and Gampaha; Central Province--Kandy, Matale, and Nuwara Eliya; Southern Province--Galle, Matara, and Hambantota; North-Western Province--Kurunegala and Puttalam; North-Central Province-- Anuradhapura and Polonnaruwa; Uva--Badulla and Monaragala; and Sabaragamuwa--Kegalle and Ratnapura.

21. Denham, Ceylon at the Census of 1911, pp. 197-198; Census, 1946; Census, 1981, No. 1.

22. See Census, 1981, No. 1, p. vii. Between 1971 and 1981, Indian Tamils declined as a proportion of the population of Nuwara Eliya district in the Central Province from 52.3 to 47.3 percent, while Sri Lanka Tamils increased from 4.1 to 13.5 percent (1971 General Report, p. 84; Census, 1981, No. 1, p. 10). However, prior to the latter census the boundaries of Nuwara Eliya district were altered, complicating the task of interpreting these data.

23. On the ubiquity of separatist movments in the modern world, see D.N. MacIver, "Conclusion: Ethnic Identity and the Modern State," in Colin H. Williams, ed., National Separatism (Vancouver, Canada: University of British Columbia Press, 1982), pp. 299-307.

24. Although the census figures do not indicate religion by ethnic community, examination of the sizes of ethnic and religious groups in the region suggests that nearly 190,000 Tamil Christians were located in the six districts in 1981, of whom about 104,000 were in Jaffna and 30,000 in Mannar. These calculations are based on the assumptions that almost all Buddhists were Sinhalese (there have been some conversions to Buddhism among Tamil "untouchable" castes), nearly all non-Buddhist Sinhalese and nearly all Burghers were Christians, and virtually all

120

Hindus were Sri Lanka or Indian Tamils. The number of Christians who were presumed not to be Sinhalese or Burghers is close to the number of Tamils (Sri Lanka and Indian) less the number of Hindus for each district. The "other" categories for both ethnic group and religion complicate the calculation but the numbers involved are very small. Presumably the "other" ethnic category includes some members of the so-called Indian Moor community who are Muslims and could help to explain the slightly larger total of Muslims than of Sri lanka Moors and Malays in each of the districts. The calculations are based on Census, 1981, No. 1, p. 3.

25. For example, Government of Sri Lanka, Sri Lanka-- Who Wants a Separate State? (Colombo: Department of Information, 1983).

26. See Bryan Pfaffenberger, "The Cultural Dimension of Tamil Separatism in Sri Lanka," Asian Survey, XXI (November 1981), pp. 1145-1157; and K. Sivathamby, "Some Aspects of the Social Composition of the Tamils of Sri Lanka," in Ethnicity and Social Change in Sri Lanka (Colombo: Social Scientists' Association, 1984), pp. 121-145.

27. An argument for marked and widening political differences between Batticaloa and the northern districts, based on analysis of election results in 1977 and 1982 (before the escalation of violence in 1983-1984), is made by M.P. Moore, "The 1982 Elections and the New Gaullist-Bonapartist State in Sri Lanka," in Manor, ed., Sri Lanka in Change and Crisis, especially pp. 65-67. On the growth of support for separatism among Tamil Catholics see, in the same volume, R.L. Stirrat, "The Riots and the Roman Catholic Church in Historical Perspective," especially pp. 203-204.

5

Future Research
and Policy Implications

The chapters in this volume take internal migration in Sri Lanka as a starting point for the analysis of related social phenomena: unbalanced sex ratios and spouse separation, the rise in suicide, and the continuing problem of ethnic conflict. Each of these issues is extremely complicated. Our analysis is far from exhaustive but can provide a basis and an impetus for further urgently needed work on these topics from a range of perspectives. This chapter first provides a brief review of our findings, then a discussion of some of the most pressing areas for future research that were exposed in the process of our explorations of the census and other data, and lastly some implications for public policy.

The presentation of the general pattern of internal migration in Sri Lanka in Chapter 1 sets the stage for the following chapters. Compared to many other developing nations whose internal migration is dominated by flows to primate urban centers, the predominant pattern in Sri Lanka is rural-to-rural movement, although Colombo of course receives large numbers of migrants. The dominant flow of migrants has been from the crowded southwestern Wet Zone northerly and easterly into the sparsely populated Dry Zone, impelled by a post-1945 surge of population growth and encouraged by government irrigation projects and settlement schemes.

A possible "risk factor" for migrants' adjustment processes and overall social harmony in destination zones is posited in Chapter 2 to be extremely male-preponderant sex ratios. Although a determinant role of sex ratios in creating psychological and social disruption cannot be established on the basis of the census data, strong suggestions about the potentially most vulnerable districts and age groups can be made. A variety of data examined on sex ratios in the district populations, numbers of male and female migrants in eleven selected districts, and certain sociocultural variables all point to the greatest potential migration-related "stress points" to be the prime adult years for both males and females in the Dry Zone districts.

The analysis of suicide data in Chapter 3 reveals a dramatic increase in the rates of suicide for both males and females in recent decades. The relationship between internal migration patterns and suicide appears to be strong in many districts, particularly those of the Dry Zone where male and female suicides are among the very highest in Asia. Nevertheless, suicide is too broad and complex a phenomenon to be neatly explained by a single factor such as population movement. While the rise has been less spectacular, the suicide rate has increased in all areas of the island, even where migration is not significant. Suicides apparently have increased in all ethnic groups, but perhaps are especially difficult to relate to migration in the case of the Tamil population of the far North. Overall, in a situation where large proportions of the population are resident in a district other than that of their birth, one can point to a general state of social upheaval that must bring with it psychological stress of varying degress. Suicide is, of course, one of the most extreme expressions of such stress.

The ethnic conflict and violence that has flared in recent decades is, like the rising incidence of suicide, not explicable in terms of any single causal factor. Nonetheless, the movement of Sinhalese migrants into northern and eastern districts considered by many Sri Lanka Tamils to be part of the traditional Tamil homeland on the island has provided one emotion-laden issue in the contest between ethnic communities and has without doubt helped to fuel the rising communal strife. Migration has brought Sinhalese north and east and Tamils south to populate once nearly empty Dry Zone areas, heightening the potential for confrontation and conflict between communities. Although many issues divide the political spokesmen of the two communities, the demand for a separate Tamil state has dramatized the territorial dimension of the conflict and has underscored the complexities of territorial delimitation of ethnic communities.

PROSPECTIVE RESEARCH DIRECTIONS

The core chapters of this volume--on sex ratios, suicide, and ethnic conflict--all raise important questions that cannot be answered by census data or currently available knowledge, as far as we are aware. In this section several major issues are presented in hope that future researchers will be inspired to investigate them.

Chapter 2 brought to the surface a variety of intriguing and serious research questions. Why has the general government policy of family migration into Dry Zone settlement schemes not been followed, with the result that numerous males relocate without wives? What is life like for residents of the towns and rural areas in the Dry Zone where, in some urban areas, males outnumber females 2:1 in selected age groups? In contrast, what are the factors that bring lone females as migrants to Wet Zone south-coast districts, and what are their lives like? Do female migrants to the Wet Zone find more rewarding employment than male or female migrants to the Dry Zone? Do female migrants to the Wet Zone have a greater propensity than male or female migrants to the Dry Zone to form solidarity groups, or to discover other forms of social and psychological support? All of these questions are researchable through carefully designed microlevel surveys and/or lengthy participant observation in selected locales.

In Chapter 3, the high quality data on suicides and those of the census reports provide a good backdrop upon which more detailed studies can be designed to ask specific questions. Most importantly the social characteristics of those who commit or attempt suicide should be a subject of inquiry. What is the economic status, household background, marital status, educational level, and ethnic community of these persons? Were they migrants or indigenous to the area? If they were migrants, how recently had they moved? These questions are not easy to research since in any locale, numbers are small and potential informants difficult to locate, and the subject matter for interviews very sensitive. In the case of completed suicides, the prime informant cannot tell his/her story. Clues to suicide patterns could be provided, however, in a wider study of the "epidemiology of mental health" including attention to the social distribution of symptoms of disturbed mental health such as depression and hypertension. In this way, survey data could point to groups in the population at higher risk of committing suicide.

The tragic drama of ethnic conflict in Sri Lanka is
currently being played out in an environment that appears
singularly inconducive to dispassionate scholarship. The
recent proclivity to rewrite history to support one
communal contention or another is a sad side effect of the
bitter inflammation of communal relations. Some
encouragement may, however, be taken from the continuing
staunch objectivity--emotionless detachment may be too much
to ask--of some scholars of both major communities and the
activities of a few institutions such as the Marga
Institute and the International Centre for Ethnic Studies,
even in investigating questions laden with contention and
emotion. Arguments regarding the traditional Tamil
homeland, from both Tamil and Sinhalese partisans, seem too
often to be based on sketchy and woefully simplistic
historical understanding. Painstaking historical research
and judicious evaluation of evidence might reveal a
political complexity and fluidity that would render
irrelevant the claims based on interpretations of early
history zealously being promoted on both sides of the
ethnic contest.

In a quite different area of scholarly concern,
migrant settlements have been viewed as hotbeds of communal
hostility and political volatility since the first
Sinhalese-Tamil riots in the Gal Oya settlement area in
1956. Yet, little empirically grounded research has
appeared to illuminate the sociopolitical dynamics of the
settlements, the political and ethnic violence they
alledgedly foment, or the impact of migration on patterns
of authority and mechanisms of social control,
understanding of which could cast much needed light on the
social and political implications of migration. Finally,
historically and contemporaneously many instances are known
of amicable and cooperative daily interactions between
members of different ethnic groups living in close
proximity within particular localities. Surely, much
important information could be obtained by careful study of
the circumstances that allow or facilitate such
interactions in some localities and times but not in
others. It can scarcely be doubted by any but the most
passionate zealot or the most despairing cynic that
rigorous scholarly objectivity and concern with the
evidence uncovered, without regard for the communal
debating points gained or lost, on topics such as these we
have specified can contribute to knowledge of ethnic

interactions which just might prevent a recurrence of the slide into the pit of ethnic bitterness that Sri Lanka has experienced.

PUBLIC POLICY CONSIDERATIONS

The exposure of these unintended consequences of internal migration--unbalanced sex ratios, rising rates of suicide, and ethnic conflict--carries with it some implications for public policy. Because internal migration is not the sole determining factor of rising suicide rates and ethnic tension, however, any migration policy suggestions in these areas are necessarily tentative.

In terms of unbalanced sex ratios as a potential social problem, public policy makers should first be aware of the extreme degree of male preponderance which is particularly pronounced in the Dry Zone. Efforts to promote migration of families as units should be increased and attempts to reunite families living in separation should be considered. The census data on employment, as well as several case studies, document that female opportunities for employment in the Dry Zone are extremely low compared to other parts of the island. Serious efforts to develop opportunities for female employment in the region should be made, perhaps with insights gained as to appropriate projects from studies of women's work made in the Wet Zone. Increased employment options for women in the Dry Zone may encourage more whole-family migration.

The suicide data reveal that Sri Lanka is now among the nations of the world with high rates of suicide. Other Asian nations have developed various programs for suicide prevention. Policy options could take two major directions, one based on our research findings, that seeks to alter the social dynamics leading to suicide, and the other that simply provides psychological/counselling services for individuals without attempting to change the social background. Probably each tack is necessary for short-run and long-run amelioration of the problem.

The problems associated with ethnic confrontation appear especially intractable and involve many issues and questions well beyond the scope of this study. It seems to us pointless for Sinhalese or Tamil spokesmen to argue whether residents of a particular locality 800 years ago were Sinhalese or Tamil or whether 1,000-year-old ruins were once a Buddhist or a Hindu shrine. The need for greater sensitivity for social consequences of government-sponsored or facilitated movements of population, including the ethnic composition of settlements and their neighboring areas, is too obvious to require mention. The depth of the communal gulf that has opened over recent decades suggests that public policies regarding internal migration alone cannot have a decisive impact on the course of the ethnic struggle. Also, some major part of the migration that has occurred has resulted from many individual decisions not made in response to public enticements. Population growth has probably had more to do with changing the demographic face of Sri Lanka than any public policy decision. Presumably, much could be done to create and publicize economic advantages to prior residents of development accompanying settlement of an area, and to make evident to migrants the advantages of harmonious relations with the earlier residents as well as with other migrants of different ethnic affiliation. As a minimal step in reducing the explosiveness of migration as an issue in the Sinhalese-Tamil confrontation, it seems vital that public officials carefully avoid the threat of flooding areas with Sinhalese migrants in an effort to intimidate separatist opponents no matter how violent or disruptive they may be. Still, resolution of migration-related issues in the current conflict of ethnic communities must come as a part of a much broader resolution of many complex and difficult problems.

IN CONCLUSION

This book brings together discussions of important issues in Sri Lanka's recent history--aspects of social change that are related to large-scale population movement. In many ways, Sri Lanka appears as a unique case of a richly endowed land afflicted with surprisingly high levels of social disruption. Nevertheless, Sri Lanka has important affinities with other Asian nations, especially those experiencing rapid social change, so that lessons learned in Sri Lanka may have relevance beyond its borders. The experience of Sri Lanka can, at the very least, raise a number of searching questions regarding unanticipated and undesirable concomitants of social transitions in other contemporary nations undergoing swift and extensive change.

These chapters highlight the more depressing and worrisome sides of life in modern Sri Lanka as they appear linked with internal migration. This perspective is offered in the hope that knowledge and understanding of social problems contribute, even if slowly, to their resolution.

Bibliography

Abeysekera, Dayalal. "Regional Patterns of Intercensal and Lifetime Migration in Sri Lanka." Papers of the East-West Population Institute, No. 75. Honolulu, HI: East-West Population Institute, 1981.

_____. "Rural to Rural Migration in Sri Lanka," in Calvin Goldscheider, ed., Rural Migrants in Developing Nations: Comparative Studies of Korea, Sri Lanka, and Mali. Boulder, CO: Westview Press, 1984, pp. 109-208.

Abhayaratne, O. E. R., and C. H. S. Jayewardene. "Internal Migration in Ceylon," Ceylon Journal of Historical and Social Studies, VIII, 1965, pp. 68-90.

All Party Conference (Sri Lanka). "Annexure C," Statement of His Excellency the President and Chairman of the All Party Conference. Colombo: All Party Conference Secretariat, Dec. 14, 1984.

Boserup, Ester. Woman's Role in Economic Development. New York: St. Martin's Press, 1970.

Bowles, John R. "Suicide and Attempted Suicide in Contemporary Western Samoa," in Francis X. Hezel, Donald H. Rubenstein and Geoffrey M. White, eds., Culture, Youth and Suicide in the Pacific: Papers from an East-West Center Conference. Working Paper Series, Pacific Islands Studies Program. Honolulu, HI: University of Hawaii at Manoa and the Institute of Culture and Communication, East-West Center, 1985, pp. 15-35.

Brown, Alan, and Egon Neuberger, eds. Internal Migration: A Comparative Perspective. New York: Academic Press, 1977.

Burke, A. W. "Socio-Cultural Determinants of Attempted Suicide among West Indians in Birmingham: Ethnic Origin and Immigrant Status," British Journal of Psychiatry, CIXXX, 1976, pp. 261-266.

Burvill, P. W., et al. "Attempted Suicide and Immigration in Perth, Western Australia, 1969-1978," Acta Psychiatrica Scandinavica, LXIIX, 1983, pp. 89-99.

Bussaratid, Somporn, and Sompop Ruangtrakool. "Thailand," in Lee Headley, ed., Suicide in Asia and the Near East. Berkeley: University of California Press, 1983, pp. 142-166.

Central Bank of Ceylon. Annual Report of the Monetary Board to the Hon. Minister of Finance and Planning for the Year 1977. Colombo: Central Bank of Ceylon, 1978.

Central Bank of Ceylon. Department of Economic Research. Survey of Economic Conditions in the Mahaweli Development Area, 1974. Colombo: Central Bank of Ceylon, 1975.

Connell, John, Biplab Dasgupta, Roy Laishley, and Michael Lipton. Migration from Rural Areas: The Evidence from Village Studies. Delhi: Oxford University Press, 1976.

Denham, E. B. Ceylon at the Census of 1911. Colombo: Government Printer, 1912.

Department of Census and Statistics (Sri Lanka). Census of Ceylon, 1946. Colombo: Government Press. Vol. I, Part 1, 1950. Vol. I, Part 2, 1951. Vol. IV, 1952.

_____. Census of Population, Ceylon, 1963. Vol. I, Part 1. Colombo: Government Press, 1967.

_____. Census of Population and Housing, Sri Lanka, 1981. Preliminary Release No. 1. Colombo: Department of Census and Statistics, 1981.

_____. Census of Population and Housing, Sri Lanka, 1981: The Economically Active Population, Tables Based on a Ten Percent Sample. Preliminary Release No. 4. Colombo: Department of Census and Statistics, 1983.

_____. Census of Population and Housing, Sri Lanka, 1981: Population Tables Based on a Ten Percent Sample. Preliminary Release No. 2. Colombo: Department of Census and Statistics, 1982.

_____. Census of Poulation, 1971. Vol. II, Part 1. Colombo: Department of Government Printing, 1975.

_____. Census of Population 1971, Sri Lanka: General Report. Colombo: Department of Census and Statistics, 1978.

_____. 1971 Census of Population. Vol. I, Parts 1-22. Mimeographed; Colombo: Department of Census and Statistics, 1974.

_____. The Population of Sri Lanka. Colombo: Department of Census and Statistics, 1974.

_____. Socio-Economic Survey of Sri Lanka, 1969-70, Rounds 1-4. Vol. I. Colombo: Department of Census and Statistics, 1973.

_____. Statistical Abstract of Sri Lanka [title varies]. Colombo: Department of Government Printing, annual.

DeVos, George. "Ethnic Pluralism: Conflict and Accommodation," in George DeVos and Lola Romanucci-Ross, eds., Ethnic Identity: Cultural Continuities and Change. Palo Alto, CA: Mayfield Publishing Company, 1975, p. 5-41.

Dissanayake, S. A. W., and Padmal de Silva. "Sri Lanka," in Lee Headley, ed., Suicide in Asia and the Near East. Berkeley: University of California Press, 1983, pp. 167-209.

Dissanayake, S. A. W., and W. P. de Silva. "Suicide and Attempted Suicide in Sri Lanka," Ceylon Journal of Medical Science, XXIII, June and December 1974, pp. 10-17.

Divale, William, and Marvin Harris. "Population, Warfare, and the Male Supremacist Complex," American Anthropologist, LXXVIII, 1976, pp. 521-538.

D'Souza, Stan, and Lincoln C. Chen. "Sex Differentials in Mortality in Rural Bangladesh," Population and Development Review, VI, June 1980, pp. 257-270.

Durkheim, Emile. Suicide: A Study in Sociology. Glencoe, IL: Free Press, 1951.

Dyson, Tim, and Mick Moore. "On Kinship Structure, Female Autonomy, and Demographic Behavior in India," Population and Development Review, IX, March 1983, pp. 35-60.

El-Badry, M. A. "Higher Female Than Male Mortality in Some Countries of South Asia: A Digest," Journal of the American Statistical Association, LXIV, December 1969, pp. 1234-1244.

Farmer, B. H. Pioneer Peasant Colonization in Ceylon. London: Oxford University Press, 1957.

Fawcett, James T., Siew-Ean Khoo, and Peter C. Smith, eds. Women in the Cities of Asia: Migration and Urban Adaptation. Boulder, CO: Westview Press, 1984.

Fernando, Dallas F. S. "Changing Nuptiality Patterns in Sri Lanka," Population Studies, IXXX, 1975, pp. 179-190.

Gaminiratne, K. H. W. "Some Aspects of Urbanization in Sri Lanka." Occasional Paper No. 3. Colombo: Ministry of Information and Broadcasting and UNESCO/UNFPA, 1976.

Goldscheider, Calvin, ed. Rural Migrants in Developing Nations: Comparative Studies of Korea, Sri Lanka, and Mali. Boulder, CO: Westview Press, 1984.

_____. Urban Migrants in Developing Nations: Patterns and Problems of Adjustment. Boulder, CO: Westview Press, 1983.

Government of Sri Lanka. Northern Terrorists Massacre Innocent Farmer Civilians in Sri Lanka. Leaflet; no facts of publication.

_____. Report of the Presidential Commission of Inquiry into the Incidents Which Took Place Between 13th August and 15th September, 1977. Sessional Paper VII--1980. Colombo: Department of Government Printing, 1980.

_____. Sri Lanka--Who Wants a Separate State? Colombo: Department of Information, 1983.

Gulati, Leela. "Impacts of Male Migration to the Middle East on the Family: Some Evidence from Kerala." Working Paper No. 76. Trivandrum, Kerala: Centre for Development Studies, 1983.

Hackenberg, Robert A., et al. "Migration, Modernization and Hypertension: Blood Pressure Levels in Four Philippine Communities," Medical Anthropology, VII, 1983, pp. 44-71.

Hallet, Robin. "Desolation on the Veld: Forced Removals in South Africa," African Affairs, LXXXIII, 1983, pp. 301-320.

Havighurst, Robert H. "Suicide and Education," in Edwin S. Schneidman, ed., On the Nature of Suicide. San Francisco, CA: Jossey-Bass, 1969, pp. 53-67.

Headley, Lee, ed. Suicide in Asia and the Near East. Berkeley: University of California Press, 1983.

Hemasiri, H. G. D. "Demographic Factors in Agricultural Development--Sri Lanka's Experience," Staff Studies, Central Bank of Ceylon, VII, September 1977, pp. 71-91.

Jones, Gavin W., and S. Selvaratnam. Population Growth and Economic Development. Colombo: Hansa Publishers, 1972.

Kakar, Sudhir. The Inner World: A Psychoanalytic Study of Childhood and Society in India. 2nd ed.; New York: Oxford University Press, 1981.

Kearney, Robert N. "Ethnic Conflict and the Tamil Separatist Movement in Sri Lanka," Asian Survey, XXV, September 1985, pp. 898-917.

Kearney, Robert N., and Barbara D. Miller. "Sex Differences in Patterns of Internal Migration in Sri Lanka," Women in International Development Working Paper Series No. 44. East Lansing, MI: Michigan State University, Office of Women in International Development, 1984.

Kearney, Robert N., and Barbara D. Miller. "Sex-Differential Patterns of Internal Migration in Sri Lanka," Peasant Studies, Summer 1983, pp. 224-250.

Kearney, Robert N., and Barbara D. Miller. "The Spiral of Suicide and Social Change in Sri Lanka," Journal of Asian Studies, XLV, November 1985, pp. 81-101.

Kelly, Narinder Oberoi. "Some Socio-Cultural Correlates of Indian Sex Ratios: Case Studies of Punjab and Kerala." Unpublished doctoral dissertation, University of Pennsylvania, 1975.

Langford, Christopher M. "Fertility Change in Sri Lanka Since the War: An Analysis of the Experience of Different Districts," Population Studies, XXXV, 1981, pp. 285-306.

_____. "The Fertility of Tamil Estate Workers in Sri Lanka." No. 31. London: World Fertility Survey, 1982.

_____. "Sex Differentials in Mortality in Sri Lanka: Changes Since the 1920s," Journal of Biosocial Science, XVI, 1984, pp. 399-410.

Lester, D. "Migration and Suicide," Medical Journal of Australia, I, 1972, pp. 941-942.

Lund, Raghnild. "Women and Development Planning in Sri Lanka," Geografiska Annaler, LXIII, 1981, pp. 95-108.

MacIver, D. N. "Conclusion: Ethnic Identity and the Modern State," in Colin H. Williams, ed., National Separatism. Vancouver, Canada: University of British Columbia Press, 1982, pp. 299-307.

Macpherson, Cluny, and La'avasa Macpherson. "Suicide in Western Samoa: A Sociological Perspective," in Francis X. Hezel, Donald H. Rubenstein and Geoffrey M. White, eds., Culture, Youth and Suicide in the Pacific: Papers from an East-West Center Conference. Working Paper Series, Pacific Islands Studies Program. Honolulu, HI: University of Hawaii at Manoa and the Institute of Culture and Communication, East-West Center, 1985, pp. 36-73.

134

Manor, James, ed. Sri Lanka in Change and Crisis. New York: St. Martin's Press, 1984.

Maslow, Abraham H. The Farther Reaches of Human Nature. New York: Viking Press, 1971.

Miller, Barbara D. The Endangered Sex: Neglect of Female Children in Rural North India. Ithaca, NY: Cornell University Press, 1981.

Miller, Barbara D., and Robert N. Kearney, "Women's Suicide in Sri Lanka," in Patricia Whelehan, ed., The Anthropology of Women's Health. South Hadley, MA: Bergin and Garvey Publishers, forthcoming.

Ministry of State (Sri Lanka). The Thimpu Talks: The Stand Taken by the Sri Lanka Government. Colombo: Department of Information, 1985.

Moore, M. P. "The 1982 Elections and the New Gaullist-Bonapartist State in Sri Lanka," in James Manor, ed., Sri Lanka in Change and Crisis. New York: St. Martin's Press, 1984, pp. 51-75.

Murray, Colin. Families Divided: The Impact of Migrant Labour in Lesotho. New York: Cambridge University Press, 1981.

Nadarajah, T. "The Transition from Higher Female to Higher Male Mortality in Sri Lanka," Population and Development Review, IX, June 1983, pp. 317-325.

Obeyesekere, Gananath. The Goddess Pattini and the Parable on Justice. Punitham Tiruchelvam Memorial Lecture, July 21, 1983. Colombo: New Leela Press, 1983.

Papanek, Hanna. "Men, Women and Work: A Comparison of Separate Worlds in Muslim South Asia and Two-Person Careers in America." Occasional Paper Series, Muslim Studies Sub-Committee of the Committee on Southern Asia Studies. Chicago, IL: University of Chicago, 1972.

Paranavitana, Cyril. "Land Hunger, Agrarian Changes and Government Policies: A Comparative Study of Nine Villages in Sri Lanka, 1955 & 1980," Marga (Colombo), VIII, 1985, pp. 22-39.

Parliament (Sri Lanka). Parliamentary Debates (Hansard), Official Report. Vol. 34, 1985.

Peiris, Gerald. "The Physical Environment," in K. M. de Silva, ed., Sri Lanka: A Survey. Honolulu: University Press of Hawaii, 1977, pp. 3-30.

Pfaffenberger, Bryan. "The Cultural Dimension of Tamil Separatism in Sri Lanka," Asian Survey, XXI, November 1981, pp. 1145-1157.

"Political Resolution Unanimously Adopted at the 1st
National Convention of the Tamil Liberation Front Held
at Pannakam (Vaddukoddai Constituency) on 14.5.1976,
Presided over by Mr. S.J.V. Chelvanayakam, Q.C., M.P."
Mimeographed.

Ponnambalam, Satchi. Sri Lanka: National Conflict and the
Tamil Liberation Struggle. London: Zed Books, 1983.

Presidential Address of Mr. S.J.V. Chelvanayagam, K.C., Delivered at the Inaugural and First Business Meeting of
the Ilankai Tamil Arasu Kadchi (The Federal Freedom
Party of the Tamil-speaking People of Ceylon) on 18th
December, 1949, at the G.C.S.U. Hall, Colombo. Colombo: Ilankai Tamil Arasu Kadchi, n.d.

Preston, Samuel H. Mortality Patterns in National
Populations--With Special Reference to Recorded Causes
of Death. New York: Academic Press, 1976.

Resnick, H. L. P. "Suicide," in Harold I. Kaplan, Alfred
M. Freedman, and Benjamin J. Sadock, eds., Comprehen-
sive Textbook of Psychiatry. 3rd ed.; Baltimore, MD:
Williams and Wilkins, 1980, Vol. II, pp. 2085-2098.

Richmon, Anthony H., and Daniel Kubat. Internal Migration:
The New World and the Third World. Beverly Hills, CA:
Sage Publications, 1976.

Risseuw, Carla. The Wrong End of the Rope: Women Coir
Workers in Sri Lanka. Leiden: University of Leiden
Research and Documentation Center on Women and
Development, 1980.

Schrijvers, Joke. Mothers for Life: Motherhood and Marginalization in the North Central Province of Sri
Lanka. Delft, Netherlands: Eburon, 1985.

Selvadurai, A. J. "Kinship and Land Rights in the Context
of Demographic Change," in James Brow, ed., Population, Land and Structural Change in Sri Lanka and
Thailand. Leiden: E. J. Brill, 1976, pp. 97-112.

Shkilnyk, Anastasia M. A Poison Stronger Than Love: The
Destruction of an Ojibwa Community. New Haven, CT:
Yale University Press, 1985.

Shue, Tuck Wong. "Net Migration and Agricultural Change in
Sri Lanka," in R. B. Mandal, ed., Frontiers in Migration Analysis. New Delhi: Concept, 1981, pp. 439-
454.

Sivathamby, K. "Some Aspects of the Social Composition of
the Tamils of Sri Lanka," in Ethnicity and Social
Change in Sri Lanka. Colombo: Social Scientists'
Association, 1984, pp. 121-145.

Skjønsberg, Else. A Special Caste? Tamil Women of Sri

Lanka. London: Zed Press, 1983.

Sopher, David E. "Female Migration in Monsoon Asia: Notes from an Indian Perspective," _Peasant Studies_, X, Summer 1983, pp. 289-300.

Speare, Alden, Jr. "Methodological Issues in the Study of Migrant Adjustment," in Calvin Goldscheider, ed., _Urban Migrants in Developing Nations: Patterns and Problems of Adjustment_. Boulder, CO: Westview Press, 1983, pp. 21-42.

Stirrat, R. L. "The Riots and the Roman Catholic Church in Historical Perspective," in James Manor, ed., _Sri Lanka in Change and Crisis_. New York: St. Martin's Press, 1984, pp. 196-213.

Strauch, Judith. "Women in Rural-Urban Circulation Networks: Implications for Social Structural Change," in James T. Fawcett, Siew-Ean Khoo, and Peter C. Smith, eds., _Women in the Cities of Asia: Migration and Urban Adaptation_. Boulder, CO: Westview Press, 1984, pp. 60-77.

Straus, Jacqueline H., and Murray A. Straus. "Suicide, Homicide, and Social Structure in Ceylon," _Journal of Sociology_, LVIII, March 1953, pp. 461-469.

"A Survey of Employment, Unemployment and Underemployment in Ceylon," _International Labour Review_, LXXXVII, March 1963, pp. 247-257.

Tambiah, S. J. _Sri Lanka: Ethnic Fratricide and the Dismantling of Democracy_. Chicago: University of Chicago Press, 1986.

Tamil Refugees Rehabilitation Organisation. _Communal Disturbances in Sri Lanka_. Mimeographed; no place or publisher, 1980.

Terrorism in North Sri Lanka and Racial Riots: An Analysis of Their Causes. Colombo: World Fellowship of Buddhists Sri Lanka Regional Centre, n.d. [1983].

Todaro, Michael P. _Internal Migration in Developing Countries: A Review of Theory, Evidence, Methodology and Research Priorities_. Geneva: International Labour Office, 1976.

United Nations. Economic and Social Commission for Asia and the Pacific. _Migration, Urbanization and Development in Sri Lanka_. New York: United Nations, Comparative Study on Migration, Urbanization and Development in the ESCAP Region, Country Report, ST/ESCAP/211, 1980.

Visaria, Pravin M. "Sex Ratios at Birth in Territories with a Relatively Complete Registration," _Eugenics_

Quarterly, XIV, 1967, pp. 132-142.

_____. The Sex Ratio of the Population of India. Census of India, Vol. I, Monograph X. Delhi: Office of the Registrar General, 1961.

Western, John. Outcast Cape Town. London: George Allen & Unwin, 1981.

Waldron, Ingrid. "The Role of Genetic and Biological Factors in Sex Differences in Mortality," in Alan Lopez and Lado Ruzicka, eds., Sex Differentials in Mortality: Trends, Determinants, and Consequences. Department of Demography, Miscellaneous Series No. 4. Canberra, Australia: Australian National University, 1983, pp. 141-164.

Wolf, Diane. "Female Employment, Fertility and Survival Strategies in Sri Lanka." Staff Paper No. 80-16. Ithaca, NY: Department of Agricultural Economics, Cornell University, 1980.

Wood, A. L. Crime and Aggression in Changing Ceylon, in Transactions of the American Philosophical Society, New Series, Vol. VI, Part 8. Philadelphia: American Philosophical Society, 1961.

Index

All Party Conference, 95

Amparai district, 3, 4, 6 (map), 7, 9, 11, 13, 14, 15, 17 (map), 19-22, 25, 31, 43, 45, 47, 54, 56, 70, 72-75, 86, 92, 93, 96-101, 102, 103, 104 (map), 105 (map), 106, 110, 114, 119 (n20)

Anuradhapura district, 4, 6 (map), 7, 8, 9, 11, 13, 14, 15, 17 (map), 19-22, 25, 31, 43, 46, 47, 49, 54, 56, 58, 60, 67, 70, 72, 73, 74, 75, 80, 82, 93, 103, 106, 108, 119 (n20)

Badulla district, 4, 6 (map), 7, 9, 11, 13, 15, 17 (map), 19-22, 25, 31, 43, 53, 54, 70, 73, 75, 93, 106, 119 (n20)

Batticaloa district, 4, 5, 6 (map), 7, 9, 11, 13, 15, 17 (map), 19-22, 25, 31, 44, 53, 54, 56, 57, 70, 73, 75, 80, 81, 83, 92, 93, 96, 97, 98, 99-101, 102-103, 104 (map), 105 (map), 106-108, 110,

Batticaloa district (cont'd), 113-115, 119 (n20), 120 (n27)

Buddhists, 92, 94-95, 113, 119-120 (n24)

Burghers, 38 (n19), 92, 119-120 (n24)

Christians, 92, 113, 119-120 (n24)

Colombo (city), 10, 29, 111, 121

Colombo district, 4, 6 (map), 7, 8, 9, 11, 13, 14, 15, 17 (map), 18-26, 31, 34, 42, 45-48, 51, 52, 54, 56-60, 67, 71-75, 88 (n12), 93, 106, 113, 116, 119 (n20)

Colonization schemes, 10, 47, 84-85, 94, 95, 98, 121, 124, 126

Communal violence, 33, 95, 98, 111, 113, 115, 116, 122

Dehiwala-Mt. Lavinia, 29

Districts
  as units of analysis, 3
  locations of, 6 (map), 17 (map)

Districts (cont'd), See also
    individual districts
Dry Zone, 5, 6 (map), 8, 10,
    14, 17 (map), 18, 23, 33,
    34, 47, 52, 53, 56, 59,
    60, 67, 72, 74, 77, 84,
    85, 94, 116, 121, 122,
    123, 125
Durkheim, Emile, 65, 86

Eelam, 94, 95, 96, 113-115.
    See also Separatism;
    Tamil homeland
Employment rates. See Labor
    participation rates
Ethnic communities
    and religion, 92, 113, 119-
    120 (n24)
    in North and East, 96-109,
    115
    location of, 92-93
    See also Communal violence;
    Sex ratios, and ethnic
    communities; Separatism;
    Tamil homeland
Ethnic violence. See Communal
    violence

Federal Party, 94

Galle (city), 29
Galle district, 4, 5, 6
    (map), 7, 8, 9, 11, 13-
    15, 17 (map), 18, 19-22,
    25, 32, 42, 45-48, 51,
    52, 54, 57, 58, 60, 67,
    71-75, 80, 81, 83, 93,
    106, 119 (n20)
Gampaha district, 3, 4, 6
    (map), 7, 8, 9, 11, 13,
    14, 24, 25, 26, 72, 73,
    76, 77, 88 (n12), 93,
    106, 119 (n20)
Hambantota district, 4, 6
    (map), 7, 9, 11, 13, 15,
    17 (map), 19-22, 25, 31,

Hambantota district (cont'd),
    33,42, 46, 54, 70, 73,
    74, 75, 93, 106, 119
    (n20)
Hindus, 92, 113, 119-120
    (n24)

Indian Moors. See Moors,
    Indian
Indian Tamils. See Tamils,
    Indian
International Centre for
    Ethnic Studies, 124

Jaffna (city), 10, 29
Jaffna district, 4, 5, 6
    (map), 7, 8, 9, 11, 13,
    14, 15, 17 (map), 18-22,
    25, 26, 27, 32, 33, 34,
    44-46, 50, 53, 54, 70,
    72, 73, 75, 80, 81, 83,
    86, 89 (n14), 92, 93, 97-
    101, 102-103, 104 (map),
    105 (map), 106-110, 113-
    116, 118 (n15), 119 (n20,
    n24)

Kalutara district, 4, 6
    (map), 7, 8, 9, 11, 13,
    14, 15, 17 (map), 19-22,
    25, 32, 42, 45, 46, 54,
    56, 57, 58, 60, 67, 70,
    72-75, 93, 106, 119 (n20)
Kandy (city), 10, 29
Kandy district, 4, 6 (map),
    7, 9, 11, 13, 14, 15, 17
    (map), 18-22, 25, 26, 32,
    42, 45, 46, 49, 52, 53,
    54, 58, 60, 70, 73, 75,
    93, 106, 119 (n20)
Kegalle district, 4, 6 (map),
    7, 8, 9, 11, 13, 14, 15,
    17 (map), 19- 22, 25, 32,
    42, 54, 67, 70, 72, 73,
    75, 80, 81, 83, 93, 106,
    119 (n20)

Kilinochchi district, 103, 115, 119
Kotte, 29
Kurunegala district, 4, 6 (map), 7, 9, 11, 13, 14, 15, 17 (map), 19-22, 25, 31, 43, 54, 70, 72, 73, 75, 93, 106, 119 (n20)

Labor participation rates, 53-56, 60, 77
Lifetime migration rates, 15-16, 18, 38 (n16), 47, 77, 81
Literacy rates, 53, 56-57

Mahaweli River development project, 10, 56, 85
Malays, 38 (n19), 92, 119-120 (n24)
Male pioneer model, 23-24, 34, 46, 47, 52-53, 59, 61 (n4)
Mannar district, 4, 6 (map), 7, 8, 9, 11, 13, 15, 17 (map), 18-22, 25, 26, 31, 33, 44, 46, 50, 53, 54, 56, 70, 72, 73, 75, 89 (n14), 92, 93, 96, 97, 99-101, 102, 104 (map), 105 (map), 106-110, 113, 114, 118 (n15), 119 (n20, n24)
Marga Institute, 124
Marriage, average age for women, 53, 57, 77
Matale district, 4, 6 (map), 7, 9, 11, 13, 14, 15, 17 (map), 19-22, 25, 31, 43, 46, 54, 58, 70, 73, 75, 93, 106, 119 (n20)
Matara district, 4, 5, 6 (map), 7, 8, 9, 11, 13, 14, 15, 17 (map), 18-23, 25, 32, 33, 42, 46, 48, 52, 53, 54, 60, 67, 70,

Matara district (cont'd), 72, 73, 75, 80, 81, 83, 93, 106, 119 (n20)
Monaragala district, 3, 4, 6 (map), 7, 9, 11, 13, 14, 15, 17 (map), 19-22, 25, 31, 43, 46, 49, 54, 70, 72-75, 80, 82, 84, 86, 89- 90 (n16), 93, 106, 119 (n20)
Moors, Indian, 38 (n19), 119-120 (n24)
Moors, Sri Lanka, 30-33, 56, 91-93, 97, 100-102, 107, 109, 110, 113-115, 119-120 (n24)
Moratuwa, 29
Mullaitivu district, 3, 4, 5, 6 (map), 7, 8, 9, 11, 13, 25, 26, 72, 73, 76, 77, 80, 81, 82, 84, 88 (n12), 89 (n14), 92, 93, 95, 96, 97, 99-103, 104 (map), 105 (map), 106-110, 114, 115, 118 (n15), 119 (n20)
Muslims, 92, 113, 119-120 (n24)

Negombo, 29
Nuwara Eliya district, 4, 6 (map), 7, 9, 11, 13, 15, 17 (map), 18-22, 25, 26, 31, 43, 45, 46, 53, 54, 58, 70, 72, 73, 75, 92, 93, 106, 119 (n20)
Polonnaruwa district, 3, 4, 5, 6 (map), 7, 9, 11, 13, 14, 15, 17 (map),19-22, 23, 25, 31, 33, 43, 45, 46, 47, 49, 51, 54, 58, 60, 67, 70, 72-75, 80, 82, 89 (n13), 93, 103, 106, 108, 119 (n20)
Population density, 5, 7-8, 10, 14, 34, 66
Population growth, 1, 5,

Population growth (cont'd),
10-12, 34, 81, 101, 103,
108, 121. See also
Suicide, and population
growth
Provinces, 109, 111, 112
(map), 119 (n20)
Puttalam district, 4, 6
(map), 7, 9, 11, 13, 15,
17 (map), 19-22, 25, 31,
37 (n8), 43, 54, 70, 73,
75, 93, 106, 119 (n20)

Ratnapura district, 4, 6
(map), 7, 9, 11, 13, 14,
15, 17 (map), 19-22, 25,
31, 42, 54, 70, 73, 75,
93, 106, 119 (n20)
Religion. See Buddhists;
Christians; Ethnic
communities, and
religion; Hindus; Muslims

Riots. See Communal
violence

Separatism, 91, 94, 95, 96,
113, 122
Sex ratios, 2, 23-24, 38
(n17)
and ethnic communities,
29-33, 34, 38 (n19, n20)
and population growth and
density, 24, 26-29
as a measure of migration,
18, 23-26, 29, 34
by age group, 40, 42-47
Sinhalese, 30-33, 81, 91-93,
94, 95, 97-103, 105, 107-
110, 113-116, 119-120
(n24), 122, 124, 125, 126
Spouse separation rates, 57-
59, 60, 84
Sri Lanka Moors. See Moors,
Sri Lanka

Sri Lanka Tamils. See
Tamils, Sri Lanka
Suicide, 2, 65-86
and age groups, 78-84
and population growth, 72-
74, 77, 81, 84, 86
district variations, 67,
70-78, 80-84, 86
gender variations, 69, 74-
78, 80-84, 86, 89-90
(n16)

Tamil homeland, 94-96, 103,
115-116, 122, 124
Tamils, Indian, 30-33, 91-93,
95, 97-103, 107, 109,
110, 113, 114, 119-120
(n18, n22, n24)
Tamils, Sri Lanka, 30-33, 53,
56, 81, 91-105, 107, 109-
111, 113, 114-116, 119-
120 (n18, n24), 122, 124,
125, 126. See also
Eelam; Separatism; Tamil
homeland
Tamil United Liberation Front
(TULF), 94
Tiger Movement, 95
Trincomalee district, 4, 6
(map), 7, 9, 11, 13, 14,
15, 17 (map), 18, 19-22,
25, 31, 38 (n20), 40, 44,
46, 49, 54, 56, 57, 70,
73, 75, 92, 93, 97, 98,
99-101, 102, 103, 104
(map), 105 (map), 106-
108, 110, 113-114, 119
(n20)

Unemployment, 8-9, 66, 77.
See also Labor
participation rates
Urbanization, 10, 13, 14,
27, 34, 109-110, 121

Vavuniya district, 4, 5, 6
(map), 7, 8, 9, 11, 13,
15, 17 (map), 18, 19-22,
25, 26, 31, 33, 40, 44-
47, 50, 54, 60, 67, 70,
72-73, 80, 81, 82, 84, 88
(n12), 89 (n14), 92, 93,
96, 97, 99-101, 102, 104
(map), 105 (map),

Vavuniya district (cont'd),
106-110, 114, 118 (n15),
119 (n20)

Wet Zone, 5, 6 (map), 8, 14,
17 (map), 18, 23, 33, 47,
52, 56, 59, 60, 67, 74,
77, 84, 94, 121, 125